for Stephanie Wood

of *Diamond: The History of a Cold-Blooded Love Affair*.
His work has appeared in *The Times, Granta* and *The
Atlantic Monthly,* among other publications. He was
born in Canada and now lives in London.

ALSO BY MATTHEW HART

Diamond: The History of a Cold-Blooded Love Affair

Matthew Hart

THE IRISH GAME

A True Story of Crime and Art

V

VINTAGE

Published by Vintage 2005

2 4 6 8 10 9 7 5 3

First published in Great Britain in 2004 by
Chatto & Windus

The passages on page 105: 'Now that the owner...temper
tantrums and all' and 'For the rest of her life...to her service'
are from *Mrs Jack*, by Louise Hall Tharp, © 1965 by Louise
Hall Tharp. Reprinted by permission of Marshall A. Tharp
and Carey Edwin Tharp.

Vintage
Random House, 20 Vauxhall Bridge Road,
London SW1V 2SA

Random House Australia (Pty) Limited
20 Alfred Street, Milsons Point, Sydney
New South Wales 2061, Australia

Random House New Zealand Limited
18 Poland Road, Glenfield,
Auckland 10, New Zealand

Random House (Pty) Limited
Endulini, 5A Jubilee Road, Parktown 2193,
South Africa

The Random House Group Limited Reg. No. 954009
www.randomhouse.co.uk/vintage

A CIP catalogue record for this book
is available from the British Library

ISBN 0 099 47457 3

Papers used by Random House are natural, recyclable
products made from wood grown in sustainable forests.
The manufacturing processes conform to the environ-
mental regulations of the country of origin

Printed and bound in Great Britain by
Cox & Wyman Limited, Reading, Berkshire

Contents

The Setup

On the morning of August 27, 2003, two men in their forties drove up to an enormous mansion called Drumlanrig Castle, in Dumfriesshire, Scotland, and paid six pounds apiece to take the tour. The house was one of the residences of the duke of Buccleuch. A great art collection hung at Drumlanrig, including paintings by Rembrandt and Holbein. But a single picture outweighed all the others in importance and value—a tiny, radiant painting by Leonardo da Vinci, the *Madonna with the Yarnwinder*. Only a few paintings in the world can be attributed with confidence to the hand of Leonardo; one of them is the *Mona Lisa*, in the Louvre in Paris, and the little Scottish picture is another. People were drawn from all over the world by the duke's *Madonna*, and so were the two men who followed the guide that Wednesday morning as she led them to the staircase hall where the Leonardo hung. Just after eleven o'clock they snatched the forty-five-million-dollar painting from the wall, rushed from the house, and got away.

Such crimes appear daring, as if the perpetrators were characters who might have been played by David Niven—urbane, catlike malefactors who rob the rich with breathtaking deftness. In fact the crimes take no special skill; art thieves steal art because it is easy.

Compared to a like amount of cash, art is pitifully vulnerable. The duke would not have hung forty-five million dollars in banknotes beside the stairs in an isolated castle for anyone with six pounds to come in and see. But it is not in the nature of art to be put away in steel vaults in well-guarded banks. Treasures hang across Europe in remote houses and churches, abbeys and libraries, and in the United States in dozens of small museums. Every year thieves steal ten billion dollars' worth of them.

When the alarm went up at Drumlanrig, police poured into the countryside. Roadblocks sprang up throughout Dumfriesshire, and helicopters scoured the terrain around the estate. When no trace of the picture could be found, art-theft experts trotted out the usual wisdom for the press: that the painting could never be sold on the open market; that the popular idea of some rich, besotted collector prepared to buy a stolen masterpiece was ridiculous; and therefore that the thieves' only reasonable hope for a reward was ransom.

In fact this list of options missed the most common fate of high-end stolen art: a vast, criminal marketplace in which pictures are readily collateralized. When a great painting is stolen, its value is immediately blazoned in the press, often as part of a headline. Any potential criminal buyer is therefore assured of two important details of an item that might come into play: authenticity and worth. He would know that in the case of a picture valued in the tens of millions of dollars, the insurers would be eager to retrieve it, whether they were still on the hook for a payout or had already compensated the owner. In many jurisdictions it is illegal to benefit thieves by paying them ransom. Ransom is paid anyway, often called a "reward for information." Criminals can happily wait for years for such a disposition, because the object has cost them nothing to acquire. Moreover—and this is crucial—the art may already have begun to pay its way. Stolen paintings are now accepted as collateral by some criminals with drugs to sell. In this way the booty functions as a currency, accepted as surety for something else of value—drugs.

The discovery that stolen art was working as a kind of cash in the criminal world was made by a team of policemen who came together for a few years to break a string of famous cases, and who brought to a close one of the strangest, longest-running sagas in the annals of art crime: the case of a Vermeer, stolen twice from the same house. The trail led not only to the destruction of a legendary criminal—Martin Cahill, "the General"—and the exposure of a dark, new trade in purloined art, but to a pair of amazing discoveries: one about the painting itself; the other about the way Vermeer worked.

Art is embedded in a world animated by both money and intellect. History and scholarship single out certain artists for veneration, and the art market expresses this judgment in terms of money. In recent times the money valuations have shot up spectacularly, and thieves have taken notice. The story that follows, which began in a great mansion in the Irish countryside, reveals what high prices have created—an underworld bazaar with a ravenous appetite for art.

The Irish Game

{ 1 }

Russborough

I N IRELAND LIES a gray stone palace, in a valley by the Wick-low Mountains. The mountains themselves are dry and deso-late, and an unfriendly wind picks its way across the heath. Little roads wind here and there in the hills, and criminals drive out from Dublin to make the place their haunt. It is a wonder that the house lay unmolested for so long in its park below the hills, tethered against the drenched green sward of Ireland.

The palace of Russborough House comes into view quite sud-denly. At a bend in the N81 from Blessington, a high wall crumbles away, and there, a quarter mile up the pasture, spreads Russbor-ough's long facade. From end to end it runs for seven hundred feet. Sometimes the sun strikes the house, and the stone glows with a sil-very light, and a kind of trumpet music seems to float in the air, proclaiming a world impossibly rapturous and remote.

The Leesons built Russborough. Their ancestor came from England as a sergeant in the army of the prince of Orange, who laid waste the Catholic armies of James Stuart in 1690 at a battle on the River Boyne. This defeat completed the destruction of Catholic power in Ireland. After the Battle of the Boyne a long period of minority rule ensued, known as the Protestant Ascen-

I

dancy. The Leesons were part of this empowered group. They became brewers and Dublin property speculators, and prospered rapidly. They married well, applied for a patent of nobility, and after that passed promptly upward from the baronetage into the peerage, becoming earls of Milltown. All they needed was a decent house, and in 1741 they commissioned the foremost architect in Ireland, Richard Castle, to build it.

An army of laborers poured out of Dublin into County Wicklow and attacked the site. From the quarry at Golden Hill came ton upon ton of granite blocks, in carts that crept down the steep tracks and into the valley and along the muddy, rutted road. The stone was rich in mica, and it sparkled in the light. To the north of the rising house a horde of men slaved with shovels, carving the hillside into terraces. Even at a wage of a penny an hour, the years of spadework behind the mansion cost the Leesons thirty thousand pounds.

Russborough took eight years to build. One day, near its completion, the earl rode up and cast his eye around and ordered forty thousand trees. "About two miles from Ballymore Eustace," wrote a visitor, "we came to a beautiful situation, where we found a noble mansion forming into perfection." At last the Leesons moved in, and their aristocratic friends paraded out in droves. "I told you I was to see Russborough," the Countess of Kildare scribbled to a friend. "The house is really fine, and the furniture magnificent; but a frightful place."

Lady Kildare meant the view, the saturnine hills that scowled at Russborough from across the valley. It struck the Leesons' contemporaries as a bleak and empty setting for so princely a house.

The mansion was a masterpiece of the Palladian style and established the Leesons among the highest families of the land. The architect Castle had also built Carton, the Kildares' country seat, and Leinster House, the Dublin residence of the dukes of Leinster, where the Irish parliament now sits.

Russborough House (Matthew Hart)

Russborough became a great house of the Protestant Ascendancy. The estates of the Leesons' friends spread across that county as across the whole of Ireland. The earl paved his floors with marble and had his ceilings stuccoed by the Italian masters the Lafrancini brothers. The River Liffey was drawn from its course and made to drowse in fountains in view of the house before being released to resume its journey down to Dublin. Beyond the fountains rose the gloomy, swollen masses of the Wicklow hills, with dark clouds pouring over.

In a few generations the Leesons declined, until in 1902 the last of them to live at Russborough, the dowager Countess Geraldine, crated up most of the furnishings and silver, the pictures and the books, and sent them down to Dublin to the National Gallery of Ireland. When the countess died, Russborough passed to the family's heirs in England, who offered it to the Irish state, which declined the offer. The house sat empty until 1929, when Captain Denis Daly, a squire from Galway, bought it. Daly was a Catholic, and this affiliation soon brought the old, Protestant

Russborough

mansion to the attention of the world from which it had stood apart.

At the front of Russborough a pair of colonnades join the main house to the wings. The colonnades are set with niches, and the earls of Milltown had filled them with Italian marbles. Carved for a different time and place than rural, Catholic Ireland, the white statues gazed in naked nonchalance down across the pastures to the Liffey ponds. For two hundred years no one had thought to remark on this garmentless condition, or anyway, not to the Leesons; by 1930, things had changed. To protect its young republic from "noxious and corrupting influences," the Irish government established a board of censors. Heartened by this, the priest at Ballymore Eustace, whose parish included Russborough, waited until he had the miscreant Daly in the pews, then climbed into his pulpit and thundered against the statues. "The grass would grown in the door" of Russborough if the statues were not removed, Bernard Teevans, a gardener on the estate, remembered the priest telling Daly as the landowner sat in the congregation. In those days, Teevans added, the people of Ireland were "never up off their knees, praying day and night." Of Daly, Teevans said: "He was a very religious man, considering going for the priesthood. He came home from Mass and told some of the workmen to 'get those things out of here.'" Teevans recalled the wrecking party: "I had great fun knocking the heads, legs and arms off [the statues]. It was the best day's sport I had for a long time." They dumped the pieces in a shed.

Happily, the lavish interiors of Russborough escaped the censure of the parish, and it was these interiors that attracted Sir Alfred Beit, baronet, heir to a nineteenth-century South African diamond fortune. Sir Alfred had been leafing through *Country Life* looking for ways to decorate his London house, an enormous place in Kensington Palace Gardens, a stone's throw from Kensington Palace. He came across a picture of one of Russborough's fireplaces and com-

Sir Alfred and Lady Beit (Irish Times)

missioned a copy. Then, in 1952, while scouting around for a suitable home for their art collection, Sir Alfred and Lady Beit discovered that Russborough itself was up for sale, and bought it.

It would be hard to overstate the value and importance of the art collection that was now destined to move to Ireland. Sir Alfred's uncle and namesake had been a partner in Wernher, Beit & Company, diamond financiers. It was Julius Wernher and the first

Alfred Beit who bankrolled the young Ernest Oppenheimer, the man who ended up with control of De Beers Consolidated Mines, and through it, the entire diamond world. Wernher and Beit took for themselves huge stock positions in De Beers.

The two financiers began collecting paintings at the same time, matching each other Rembrandt for Rembrandt, Goya for Goya, Rubens for Rubens. They demanded the best and hired as their adviser the director of the German national gallery in Berlin. The Wernher collection passed down through the female line into the Phillips family, whose daughters married, respectively, the dukes of Westminster, Abercorn, and Roxburghe. In London the duchesses all kept house in the same mansion in Eton Square, stacked companionably one above the other in three enormous flats. The Wernher collection eventually went to their brother, who sold it. The Beit collection passed from Alfred to his brother Sir Otto, and from Sir Otto to Sir Alfred, who crated it up and shipped it across the Irish Sea.

Along with it went a treasure in silver, bronze sculpture, and antique furniture. This lode arrived in Ireland, was wedged into fleets of trucks, passed through Dublin, and threaded its way out into the lanes of Wicklow until it came to Russborough. There the Beits unpacked it all, moved in, and settled down. In terms of today's money, the treasure was worth more than two hundred million dollars, and there it was, in a drafty old house in the country. Not only that, the Beits were English—historically, reviled by the Irish as oppressors. One would have thought thieves would be parked along the road with their engines running. Yet Sir Alfred and Lady Beit lived peacefully at Russborough for twenty-two years before people started robbing them.

{ 2 }

La Pasionara

O N   A   W A R M   S P R I N G   N I G H T   in 1974, a silver-gray Ford Cortina station wagon drove out of County Kildare into neighboring Wicklow and took the road for Blessington. There were four people in the car: three Irishmen and a thirty-three-year-old British heiress named Bridget Rose Dugdale. Pictures of her then show an intense woman with flyaway hair and a tentative smile. A passionate nature drove everything she did, and to review her turbulent life is to see, in the end, a straight line that led her from her father's house to that spring night in County Wicklow.

Dugdale was born into sunlit circumstances at Yarty Farm, near Axminster, Devon. Her father, Lieutenant Colonel James Dugdale, was a millionaire entrepreneur, insurance broker, and landowner. He sent his daughter to private schools in France and Germany as well as England. She was a clever girl, breezed through her under-graduate degree at Oxford, and lectured at Bedford College. She took a Ph.D. in economics, became a feminist and left-wing advo-cate, worked briefly for the United Nations, and finally settled down to stir up hell with a rake named Walter Heaton, a north London union steward and former guardsman.

Dugdale, by Heaton's account, was brimming with vivacity.

Heaton himself was a luckless sinner who seems to have cut something of a figure. Whatever figure he cut when she met him quickly improved, because Dugdale had money and the habit of generosity. Heaton began to dress more smartly. He got his hands on a Mercedes-Benz. "She was a soft touch," a friend of Dugdale's confided. "She was robbed by everyone."

Free with her money, she spent little on herself. She affected battle dress and displayed a bravura fondness for dishevelment. Her demeanor was severe. People called her cold, an acquaintance said. "She wasn't cold. She may not have been able to iron a shirt or boil an egg, but she was very idealistic." Dugdale rooted around in the issues of the day like someone picking through a bin for a hat that would fit. She found Ireland.

To someone with an ardent nature, the pitiful chronicle of Irish history offered much. Its pages had been soaked in outrage from that day in 1169 when Norman conquerors from Britain came ashore at Baginburn in present-day County Wexford, an event that produced the later couplet: "At the creek of Baginburn, Ireland was lost and won." The winners were the Norman earls, who took less than one hundred years to subdue three-quarters of the island. The losers were the native Gaels; in the coming centuries they saw their customs and language extinguished, their religion persecuted, and their despoilers set above them by treachery, statute, and the sword.

The last pages in this eventful tale opened after World War I, when, in the British general election, Irish voters elected seventy-three members of the Sinn Féin Party. Instead of going to London to take their seats, the Sinn Féin members constituted themselves as the Dáil Éireann—the Irish parliament. They sat in Dublin on January 21, 1919, an act rightly construed by London as open rebellion. The Anglo-Irish war began.

Opposing British forces were the Irish Volunteers, who became the Irish Republican Army, or IRA. In the midst of this sporadic, vicious war, the British partitioned Ireland, granting home rule to the only Irishmen who did not want it: the six, largely Protestant counties of Ulster. This act imprisoned in a hostile state—Northern Ireland—a large minority of Catholics, some 40 percent of the population.

In the south the war raged on. Not even the treaty negotiated in 1921 brought peace: Under its terms, the British granted Ireland self-government but not a republic, and opposition to this arrangement flamed into a civil war, with elements of the IRA battling the new Irish state.

The pro-treaty forces won. Within a few decades Ireland was a republic anyway. But within it, unreconciled to Dublin's practical acceptance of the fact of Northern Ireland, lay well-armed units of the IRA. Officially outlawed, and feared and shunned by the mass of Irishmen, the IRA nonetheless encapsulated the beau ideal of a united Ireland. The Irish government in Dublin attacked and tolerated it by turn, and would not extradite to Britain Irishmen wanted for political crimes, including assaulting British soldiers and Northern Ireland's police. Into this ancient, blood-soaked saga Rose Dugdale flung herself.

In 1971, the British government began its policy of internment of IRA terrorists in Northern Ireland. The Anti-Internment League immediately sprang up in London, and Dugdale and Heaton embraced it. In 1972 they blockaded a street beside London's Pentonville Prison, declaring it a "no go" area to the police. They repeated the stunt in Londonderry, and afloat on this modest notoriety, the pair began to shuttle between London and Belfast—fresh adherents to the cause of Irish unity.

When the cost of standing everybody drinks wore out her fortune, Dugdale and Heaton decided to replenish it from the original source, and on the night of June 6, 1973, while her parents were away, Dugdale led three men, including Heaton, across

La Pasionara

the fields of her family's estate, through a pantry window, and into the sprawling west country house. They left with eighty-two thousand pounds' worth of paintings, silver, and porcelain. Dugdale fled with the hoard to Oxford, where she hid it in a friend's basement. It didn't stay there long; an associate betrayed them, and exactly four months later father confronted daughter in Exeter Crown Court.

The symbols of the wealth that was Dugdale's birthright glittered in the courtroom, placed there as Crown exhibits. There were eight oil paintings in their frames, rare Miessen figurines, and a treasure of silver. It was an eloquent display of the riches that Dugdale now despised. Her father told the court that in that year alone his daughter had come into an inheritance of ninety thousand pounds, and that forty-two thousand pounds of it had gone to her by check five days before the burglary. Dugdale burst out: "You love me and yet you hate me for what I do and what I stand for and what I gave your money and your mother's away for. You were concerned that I was squandering your wealth. You have been extremely generous. You gave me a great deal of love and you gave me money to see that I could live the way you lived."

"If you choose to throw your money out," said Colonel Dugdale, "it's none of my affair."

Dugdale's defense was that she had been returning to collect her own property from the house. Her father testified that the paintings, worth seventy-seven thousand pounds, had belonged to himself and his wife, and that the silver and porcelain were the property of a family trust from which Dugdale had resigned. In response, Dugdale, conducting her own defense, demanded to know the size of her father's fortune, including his interests at Lloyd's. When he demurred, she suggested that the Yarty Farm alone was worth three hundred thousand pounds. When the judge told her she had no right to interrogate her father, she declared in impassioned tones:

"This is a political trial. My father's life represents something alien to my own."

The jury convicted her of taking part in the burglary of Yarty Farm. "In finding me guilty," she told them, "you have turned me from an intellectual recalcitrant into a freedom fighter. I know no finer title."

Heaton went to prison for four years while Dugdale got off with a two-year suspended sentence and a five-thousand-pound fine. The judge believed she had been under Heaton's influence. Heaton would later bitterly remark that "anyone who knew how strong a personality she had would realize how ridiculous it was to claim that." Some of Heaton's sourness came from Dugdale's subsequent actions, for while Heaton stewed in prison Dugdale fell in love with an IRA soldier named Eddie Gallagher, and two months later she abandoned Heaton to his fate and followed Gallagher to Ireland.

In January of 1974, three men and a woman hijacked a helicopter in Donegal and made a bombing run over the Royal Ulster Constabulary station in Strabane. The attack failed. Dugdale and Gallagher, sought by the British in connection with the crime, escaped and fled south into the republic. They went into hiding and did not emerge until the night of April 26, when Rose Dugdale drove a silver-gray Cortina station wagon into the sleeping village of Blessington with three accomplices and a full supply of malign intent. They met the N81, turned south, and drove two miles to their destination: Russborough.

At Russborough they parked in the shadows of a row of beeches. They took out knives and screwdrivers, some nylon stockings, and a spool of electrician's tape. The men slipped on balaclavas and armed themselves with Russian-made Kalashnikov AK-47 assault rifles. Two of them put on rubber gloves. They kept close to a line of outbuildings as they approached the house, walked briskly across the gravel forecourt and up the steps. As her accomplices concealed themselves, Dugdale knocked on the door. The time was twenty past nine.

The door was opened by James Horrigan, a footman. Standing beside him was Patrick Pollard, the butler's fourteen-year-old son. They saw a pale woman with her hair in disarray, wearing jeans and an army sweater. She began to speak in French, something about a problem with her car. Horrigan recognized the word *voiture*. Pollard leaned out and saw the car parked at a distance from the house. Then Dugdale's companions sprang into view and rushed the man and boy. The bandits yelled and brandished their guns. They struck the two servants, opening a cut on Horrigan's head with the butt of a Kalashnikov. One of the raiders shoved the barrel of his rifle against Horrigan's neck and threatened to shoot him if he resisted. Another grabbed young Pollard and hustled him into the hall and ordered the boy to lead them to the occupants.

The Beits were in the library, reading. Sir Alfred, a tall man with a military bearing—he had been an officer—leaped up when the hooded men came barging in. He took a blow to the head, and blood leaked into his hair and onto his face and spattered the front of his shirt. He stayed on his feet as the intruders stormed around the room, searching for the alarms and roaring "capitalist pigs" at the Beits. Russborough was fitted with push-button alarms that needed to be triggered manually, and the Beits had not had time to set them off. The gang apparently thought the pictures themselves were rigged to alarms, which would alert the gardaí (police) at Blessington if any work was lifted from the wall without first disarming the alarm.

They also feared that some member of the staff, undetected in the vastness of the house, would alert the police. The teenage Pollard was forced to lead one of the men to the servants' quarters, where he burst in on a maid who was in the midst of taking a bath. The woman was ordered to dress hurriedly, and accompanied the gunman and Pollard back to the library. At this point Lady Beit was taken roughly from the room and down to the basement. One of the intruders waved a knife at her and threatened harm to Sir Alfred unless she revealed the whereabouts of money that they thought the Beits would have on hand. Lady Beit was terrified but tried not to show it. She told them calmly that there was no money; they bound her hand and foot and left her there.

Upstairs, the men pushed Sir Alfred to the floor and tied him up with the nylon stockings. Horrigan and Pollard were tied up too. "Sorry about this," muttered one of the men, seemingly embarrassed at manhandling the servants, "but it's got to be done." One of the gang kept the household under guard while Dugdale led the other two rapidly through the main apartments, pointing out the pictures to be taken. They pried the canvases from their frames with screwdrivers or hacked them out with knives. Dugdale collected documents from a desk. The thieves took nineteen pictures, including *Portrait of a Cavalier* by Hals, two oil paintings and a sketch by Rubens, a Velásquez, Goya's *Doña Antonia Zárate*, Gainsborough's *Portrait of Madame Baccelli*, a pair of little seventeenth-century oils by Gabriel Metsu, a pair of oils by the eighteenth-century Venetian master Francesco Guardi, and the prize of the collection: Vermeer's *Lady Writing a Letter with Her Maid*. Bundling the pictures into groups and fastening them with tape, the gang checked that the nylon stockings were knotted tightly on Sir Alfred and the others, and warned Pollard and Horrigan to make no calls. Then Dugdale and her accomplices dashed out into the night. The assault on Russborough had lasted ten minutes.

In the house, Sir Alfred and the servants waited for several minutes, until certain the intruders had left, then began to struggle to loose their bindings. It took Horrigan half an hour to get free, and he untied Sir Alfred and the others, who feared the gang had taken Lady Beit hostage when they'd fled. Sir Alfred and his staff searched the house and found her bound in the cellar, on the dirt floor. By the time Sir Alfred telephoned police, it was after ten o'clock. The greatest art theft in history was forty minutes old.

Twenty-six years later I drove out of Dublin on a raw, January day and took the N81 south to Russborough. The wind was driving rain clouds across the hills. I turned in at the road that runs up along the wall of the estate, and came to the towering gates. Russborough is open to the public now, but only in the summer. There was no chain blocking the way, so I went in for a look; I had not visited the house since 1990, when I first wrote about it. The gravel drive rises along an avenue of beech. The approach is from the east side, and the south front of the house grows into view as you emerge from the avenue. On the left is the field that runs from the palace down to the N81. A flock of sheep lifted their heads and watched me get out and crunch over the gravel with my camera.

A light burned in a window of the caretaker's wing, and one in the Beits' wing too. Sir Alfred had died in 1993, and I had understood that Lady Beit spent the winters in another of her homes. But as I got a little closer, an old lady appeared in a second-floor window and glowered out, and it was she.

I drove back into Blessington and parked in front of the pink stucco Downshire Hotel. Waiting in the carpeted lounge was Chief Superintendent Sean Feely, commander of the Garda division based at Naas, a nearby town. The Garda is the national constabulary of Ireland and polices both the cities and the countryside. There is scarcely a village in the republic that does not have its neat, white-painted Garda post with the blue light burning on the outside wall. *Garda* is also the term for a constable; *gardaí* is the plural for police, including all ranks.

Like other village Garda posts, Blessington's is under the command of a divisional superintendent based in a town—in this case Feely at Naas. But Feely's connection to the story is stronger than that: He was a newly promoted sergeant in the Blessington detachment when Dugdale robbed the Beits.

Feely retains the look of a country boy from County Roscommon. He has blue eyes and big, freckled hands and a toothy smile that crinkles his face. Twenty years earlier the stripes of his rank had barely been sewn onto his sleeve when Rose Dugdale and the IRA drove to Russborough, roughed up the Beits, and made off with the pictures. When the call came through to Blessington, the twenty-eight-year-old Feely and one of his constables piled into a car and tore out to the house. "As we came up the drive," Feely told me, "I remember saying to our man at the wheel, 'This could be big.' Well, it was the biggest robbery in the world at that time. But nobody would believe me when I called headquarters and said a million pounds' worth of paintings had been stolen. 'There's not a million pounds worth of paintings in the whole of Ireland,' they said. So I said, 'OK, make it *half* a million.'"

Within hours, Feely was pushed to the sidelines as the magnitude of the robbery dawned on the Garda brass. Estimates of the value of the stolen art leaped from one million pounds to eight million pounds in less than a day. As gardaí swarmed out into the countryside in search of the robbers, a horde of media descended on the village of Blessington. The theft drew international headlines. In Dublin the government made it plain to the Garda's top commanders that the crime was an embarrassment to the state.

Dugdale had raided the Beits on a Friday night. That weekend the gardaí swept through four hundred houses, barns, and remote cottages in County Wicklow alone. They set up roadblocks on the major roads and put a watch on every port and airfield in the country.

La Pasionara

Because the gang had called the Beits "capitalist pigs," a report circulated that the robbery was a political act. At Dublin Castle—the old center of British administration, which at the time of the robbery housed a Garda detective unit—some investigators thought the raid might have been politically motivated, but that the "capitalist" epithet was a false clue. The only politics behind the robbery, they believed, was the IRA's.

The first break came on Saturday afternoon, when a farmer named John Ryan, driving his cattle through a field in County Tipperary, found the Ford Cortina. A crime-scene squad came out from Dublin. In the car, shards of broken picture frame littered the floor. Teams of gardaí descended on the countryside, combing through the nearby ditches and hedgerows. At Blessington, a special operations center was established in the village Garda post. An appeal for information was broadcast throughout the republic, with the news that a one-hundred-thousand-pound reward for information had been posted by Lloyd's of London, Sir Alfred's insurers. Dedicated phone lines were set aside for tipsters. In the end, the second break did not come from a caller but from the Garda's own.

A detective in Dublin, dispatched to the vehicle registration office to check the ownership of the Cortina, discovered that the car had been purchased only two months earlier. Moreover, as he studied the file, the investigator noticed something odd about the registration form. The date was noted by the applicant as 10:2:74. It was an unusual notation, to separate the figures with colons. He knew he had seen it before, but where? Then he remembered. Police in Northern Ireland had circulated a report after the helicopter bombing in Strabane. The female suspect in that crime had dated a hotel register the same way, and that woman, police believed, was Dugdale.

No sooner did they have a suspect than a ransom note appeared, delivered to James White, director of the National Gallery of Ireland. As if to confirm police suspicions that the crime, like the criminal, had a political motivation, the note included with its demand for five hundred thousand pounds a parallel condition: the return to Northern Ireland of four Irish political prisoners then on a hunger strike in British jails.

For police, this was a break. They believed they had sealed the ports too fast for the robbers (and, more important, the pictures) to have escaped the country. The thieves were still in Ireland. They knew the identity of one of those thieves, Dugdale. Ireland is a small country with a homogeneous population. Dugdale was not Irish and could therefore not go to ground among the people. She also ran the risk of being betrayed. She had been once before, when a criminal named Ginger Mann, related to Heaton by marriage, had tipped police to the robbery of Dugdale's father's house. Police reasoned that Dugdale would know it could happen again, and she would therefore have decided to hide somewhere remote. The word went out to commanders in the field to search every isolated house in the republic.

This order made sense to Ned Hogan, the regional commander in west Cork. Hogan had in his command the country from the Old Head of Kinsale to Cape Clear—a ragged hem of lonely promontories stitched to the southern Irish coast. It seemed to Hogan an appealing place for a fugitive. He summoned his senior officers, and they laid their plans. They would pick their way down every track along the coast and knock on every door. Those were his orders, with the caution to gardaí to use every care; the robbers were heavily armed.

At Garda headquarters in Dublin's Phoenix Park, a special command was sifting the stream of reports that flowed in from every station in the country. "A lot of it came from informers," said Noel Conroy, at the time a detective in the Special Branch.

"The thing about that kind of information is that most of it is lies. Your man in the IRA sees a chance to give the guards a line, and he takes it."

Wading through this spate of tips, dismissing much of it, weighing what was rumored against what was known, the Garda analysts could reach no firm conclusion on which way the robbers had gone. That they were still in Ireland was the governing conviction. To the north, the police had the border under watch. The rest of the country ended at the sea. Dugdale was in there somewhere, and it was up to Hogan and the rest to find her. That was how things stood when a thirty-three-year-old sergeant named Pat O'Leary arrived in the village of Rosscarbery, west Cork, to take up his tiny command.

O'Leary is the image of a village policeman—big and steady, polite and somewhat formal. The full Irish name for the Garda is An Garda Síochána—literally, Guardian of the Peace—and O'Leary suggests exactly that. He comes from a village himself, Kilcummin, in County Kerry, the county that borders Cork on the northwest. In coming to Rosscarbery, he was returning to a part of Ireland he knew well: As a recruit, twelve years earlier, he had been posted to the town of Clonakilty, a Garda divisional headquarters eight miles east of Rosscarbery.

Rosscarbery is a picture-perfect Irish village. The houses and shops sparkle with new paint, and the streets look as if someone has been out with a mop only moments before. Vacationers pour into west Cork in the summer, attracted by villages like Rosscarbery, by the glittering sea and the hidden bays and the numberless paths that thread the coastal hills. O'Leary drove up to the crisp little Garda post with his wife and children at noon on April 28, a Sunday, a day and a half after Dugdale had fled from County Wicklow with the treasure. No great sense of urgency disturbed the hamlet. Garda William Creedon came out of the post and said hello, and helped

O'Leary unload his car at the yellow stucco semidetached house next door.

Today, when television news goes twenty-four hours a day, it seems incredible that a crime of such moment as Dugdale's would not have seized the whole of the national police, down to the last constable, and immediately driven them off to shake out every bush until they found her. But in Ireland then, there were not even teletypes in the village Garda posts. Orders came by phone or in person. The pace of life matched the antiquated infrastructure. No one suggested to O'Leary that he pass up the seven days allotted him to move his family in and settle them, and he took the full week. At the regional command in Bandon, Ned Hogan nursed the search along, supervising the steady, deliberate combing out of west Cork. O'Leary naturally kept abreast of this, following the story in the newspaper and discussing it with Creedon until, on Friday morning, May 4, a week after his arrival, he put on his uniform, walked next door to meet Creedon, and went to look for Rose Dugdale.

They began to the east, crossing the foot of Rosscarbery Bay, where the wash of the sea comes in across sandy tidal flats. White swans and geese and herring gulls dotted the shoreside waters. A weak sun made the sea glow gray. The two gardaí went in the direction of Newmills, then down along the eastern side of Rosscarbery Bay toward Galley Head. Highway maps of Ireland show no roads into the part of the peninsula the policemen searched that day. Yet there are tracks all through it, and farms and cottages secreted in ravines and hidden on slopes that pitch down toward the seaside cliffs. Creedon and O'Leary checked every one. They called at every door. No strangers were reported anywhere, and they returned to the village at the end of the day.

On Saturday morning they got going at half past nine. This time they drove west and plunged into the wild country along Tralong

La Pasionara

Bay. "Work like that is painstaking," O'Leary later explained. "It's slow. You're talking to local people. You're stopping all the time." There were always some visitors in that patch of Ireland, drawn in for a look at the Elizabethan ruins of Coppinger's Court or to traipse around the second-century monoliths of the Dromberg stone circle. O'Leary did not bother with these sites. If Dugdale had come down to the southwest, it was to hide. In the early afternoon the two gardaí came to the village of Glandore, then began to pick their way back along the sea.

The hills were yellow with furze. Daffodils crowded by the road. The fuchsia was in bloom and the briar full of songbirds. Primrose peeped from the stone fences that lined the track. Here and there they came upon a farm, and O'Leary would pull in and ask about strangers, and in this way found that Con Hayes had rented out a cottage to a Mrs. Merrimee, from London—a woman with a foreign accent, not English at all. The policemen asked how to find her. Hayes pointed the way. O'Leary and Creedon drove one hundred yards to some sheds, turned in at the lane, came slowly up a hill on a crumbling track squeezed by stone walls, past a line of derelict outbuildings, and into a cement-paved courtyard.

Not many places in the republic were farther from Russborough than that lonely, low white house. It seemed to crouch against the ground, held by the weight of the roof slates. Twenty yards in front was a line of battered firs, and forty yards past that the cliff, then nothing but the broad Atlantic. Storm petrels coasted by, and gulls, and the sea glittered for miles. A hedge crowded one side of the cottage. In front, an overgrown lawn made a tangle between the dwelling and a wind-wracked hedge. O'Leary got out of the car and knocked on the door.

A woman opened the door. O'Leary remembered her as a bit of a mess. Her hair was tumbled every which way and her sweater rumpled. She wore greasy jeans. "She wasn't surprised to see me," he later recalled. "Sure, she'd heard me shut the car door. I just asked her if she'd rented the house long. She answered in very broken English, saying no, she'd just taken it for a holiday. I remember standing in the yard and looking at her and thinking it might be her. Your sixth sense will tell you that."

O'Leary had to think fast. He'd noticed a window curtain shift, only slightly but enough to catch his eye. If this was Dugdale in front of him, members of the gang might be inside the house. The reports had said they were armed with assault rifles. O'Leary and Creedon had no gun at all. "If there'd been armed men there, they could have taken us and dumped us off the cliff," O'Leary said. He did not even have a radio. So he thanked the woman courteously and returned to the car. "I didn't drive off right away, because you wouldn't want to alarm them. We sat there for a minute or two, pretending just to chat, then I turned the car and went back down the road."

The orders put out by Hogan had stipulated that if anyone found Dugdale they must call for help. O'Leary went looking for a phone, a rarity then in rural Ireland. They thought Con Hayes, a farmer, had one, but decided against stopping there. It was too close to the cottage. There had been no car in the courtyard, but if the woman had come out the lane on foot, she'd have had a clear view to the farmhouse, and they did not want to give her cause to suspect they were going for help. They decided not to go to Glandore to phone, in case there was an IRA unit waiting in the village to support Dugdale. Instead they drove quickly back to the Garda post at Rosscarbery and called the divisional headquarters at Clonakilty.

The superintendent, summoned to the phone, immediately arranged a rendezvous with O'Leary. The Rosscarbery gardaí were to drive back to a place not far from Hayes's farm and wait for reinforcements. O'Leary and Creedon jumped back in the car and tore out of the village.

While this was happening, the suspect left the cottage and hurried to the Hayes farmhouse. Hayes knew her as the polite lady from London, who paid in advance and kept to herself. When she told him she needed to borrow his car to fetch some groceries, he readily agreed. She had already used the car, a black Morris Minor, for similar errands. He gave her the keys, and she returned briefly to the cottage, then came back down the lane and took the road to Glandore. She drove through the village and out to the main highway, at Leap, where she turned left. She was heading for the end of the world, beyond which there was nothing but the wide green sea.

At Skibbereen she took the road that leads out onto a peninsula and ends at the little fishing port of Baltimore. Probably she stopped to make a phone call on the way, then continued into Baltimore. She parked by the pier and walked out to the end.

People who saw her there remember her because they remembered the car, and also because she made a striking figure—disheveled and in haste, so obviously not a tourist, yet a stranger. She stood there on the pier, staring out to sea. Sherkin Island lies not far offshore, and beyond that Clear Island. She seemed to be waiting, as if for a boat to come into Baltimore Bay and take her off. While she was there, gardaí with machine guns were leaving Skibbereen and Bandon and Clonakilty, and racing to meet O'Leary at the rendezvous.

At the appointed place, O'Leary had just learned from a local man that Con Hayes's car had gone out the road to Glandore. He knew it would be her. He doubted that she planned to go far, since she was alone and would know that police would soon have a description of the car. When the vans of armed gardaí arrived, they parked in a lane and waited for her. She stayed on the pier for three-quarters of an hour, the wind blowing in against her.

"She came back along the road in Con's car," O'Leary said, "and we just pulled in behind her as she went past and followed her home. She didn't make any move to drive away." Dugdale parked, and the gardaí took her keys and then fanned out around the building. They opened the cottage door and went in slowly with their guns at the ready. The house was empty. They made a rapid search. In a closet they found six pictures. Thirteen more were in the trunk of Con Hayes's car. Dugdale stayed calm as they handcuffed her and put her in a car. O'Leary says she hardly spoke, mostly ignoring their questions. When she did offer some short reply, she still feigned broken English. "She wasn't offensive at all. I think she just realized the game was up."

Pat O'Leary, second from left. (Courtesy of An Garda Síochána)

La Pasionara

THE IRISH DEALT SWIFTLY with the bandit heiress. Seven weeks after the IRA left her to her fate on Baltimore pier, she stood in the dock in the Special Criminal Court in Dublin and pleaded "proudly and incorruptibly guilty" to receiving nineteen paintings stolen from Sir Alfred Beit, and knowing they were stolen. "I stand proudly here as the perpetrator of a calm political act to change the corporate conscience of a Cabinet," she declared to the court. "There will be, and there could be, no trial today. There is no court of justice that I can see, and there is no crime that I can apprehend, for where is the right of this court, your right to put us on trial, to intern us and deprive us of our freedom to fight for Ireland and the freedom of the Irish people? You have no such right!"

Rose Dugdale being driven from court on November 27, 1974, after being sentenced. (Irish Times)

Ned Hogan, left, with recovered art. (Irish Times)

They sent her to Limerick jail for nine years.

O'Leary saw her once again. It was long after that day at the cottage on the cliff, long after her stretch in prison. He was on a visit to Dublin with his wife. They were walking down Grafton Street, the pedestrian mall flanked by some of the capital's proudest merchants. As is often the case, the street was packed with strollers. "And didn't I see her walking up the street! At first I wasn't sure, and she sort of disappeared in the crowd. But then she got closer and I saw her again, and it was her—older, but her. Then she walked past and was lost in the crowd."

　　　　　　　　　　　　　　　　　　　　La Pasionara

{ 3 }

Under the Overpaint

As THE CHASE FOR DUGDALE and the art played out in the pages of the daily press, it involved the readers in an entertainment of the purest sort, unimpaired by feelings for the victim of the crime. Sir Alfred was a rich man and, as a titled Englishman, a member of a class that had tormented Ireland. "The Beits wouldn't mean much to the average Irish person," said Desmond FitzGerald, the knight of Glin. "Like many upper-class people, they were more or less alien—grand people in a big house."

The knight of Glin is himself a grand person in a big house. Glin Castle is a dreamy, white mansion on the banks of the River Shannon, where the knight's family have lived for centuries. Desmond FitzGerald is the twenty-ninth knight of Glin, and the last, because he has no son. He is a scholar of Irish art and, as the Christie's representative in Ireland, the country's leading picture dealer. Of the Beit collection, he said simply, "They were the best paintings in Ireland, and one of the top collections in the world. They were wonderful pictures."

Some were even more wonderful than others: the Goya, the Velásquez, the two Rubens, the Gainsborough, the two Guardis. But one picture stood above all these: Vermeer's *Lady Writing a Letter with Her Maid.* Among the old masters Vermeers are especially rare. Rembrandt made some six hundred works in his lifetime; Vermeer, only thirty-five, or possibly thirty-six. A ravenous public appetite for this mystifying Dutchman sprang into being in the 1990s, catapulting the painter into a kind of pop-star status. The 1995 Vermeer show at the National Gallery of Art in Washington, D.C., had crowds lined up around the block and even sleeping by the museum overnight for tickets. A senior Vermeer scholar remarked that it looked more like a rock concert than an old-master opening. When the show went to the Netherlands the following year, the tidal wave of Europeans that broke upon The Hague was dubbed "Vermeer madness." Five years later the Metropolitan Museum in New York put on "Vermeer and the School of Delft" and was mobbed.

The popularity of Vermeer coincided with a strong art market, escalating the monetary value of the paintings, the only attribute of interest to the thief. The price of a Vermeer today would run up into the hundreds of millions of dollars. Even in 1974 it was easily one of the most precious objects in the world. The only other Vermeer that remained in private hands belonged to Queen Elizabeth. Dugdale had tried to ransom the Irish Vermeer, something art thieves often try to do. She might also have attempted a sale to a rich, unscrupulous collector. Today there is a fashion among some art detectives to sneer at the possibility that in Argentina, say, or perhaps Taiwan, there dwells some twisted millionaire panting for illicit masterpieces. "But the myth of the crooked collector is not a myth," according to Laurence Massy, a Belgian art detective with graduate degrees in criminology and art history, and an appetite not only for arresting miscreants but also for understanding them. "The theft confers status on the thief, and maybe on the collector too. It might even be *better* if it is stolen."

High valuations do not give pictures meaning, but they give

meaning to the theft. The theft in turn converts this criminal electricity into repute and so gives something back to the painting. It does not harm the reputation of a picture that it has been stolen. Arthur Wheelock, Jr., the head of northern European baroque painting at the National Gallery in Washington and an organizer of the 1995 Vermeer show, calls this extra interest "part of the package."

T HE IRISH VERMEER is an example of the genre pictures at the heart of Vermeer's work: scenes of domestic life rendered with a catatonic rectitude. "At once dreamlike and real, elliptical and quotidian," one critic wrote, "Vermeer's luminous canvases freeze and magnify time. . . . daily life is stripped of its clutter and noise, the commonplace transformed into something stiller and more serene."

Johannes Vermeer was born in 1632 in the little Dutch city of Delft. His birthplace was an inn called De Vliegende Vos—The Flying Fox. His father, Reynier, had a lease on the inn and also dealt in art. Maps of Delft at this time show the location of the inn, on the Voldersgracht canal only a block from the town square. The square itself was dominated by the soaring steeple of the Nieuwe Kerk, the church that housed the greatest attraction in the whole of Holland: the tomb of William the Silent, prince of Orange. This warrior prince, an antecedent of the Protestant conqueror of Ireland, had led the fight to free his country from Catholic Spain in the late sixteenth century. An upwelling of national spirit followed this liberation, and a matching burst of economic activity propelled the Dutch into unprecedented prosperity. This resurgence fostered the so-called golden age of Dutch painting, an explosion of art that included the heavenly triumvirate of Hals, Rembrandt, and Vermeer.

It is often said of Vermeer that he created children quickly and paintings slowly. Although only eleven of his children survived, he fathered fifteen, a figure approaching half the number of the paintings he produced. By comparison, the average output of his contemporaries was a painting a week. Other than a few history paintings and a pair of landscapes, Vermeer's oeuvre consists of the core of genre pictures that have captivated modern viewers. Partly because there are so few, each of these small paintings seems familiar. For the most part they depict women—writing or reading letters, trying on jewelry, wearing amazing hats. When men are present, they seem outside the focus of painterly interest. The women are bathed in a clear northern light that pours through Vermeer's windows as through no others. A lattice of irresistible perspective draws the eye right through the picture plane.

Vermeer's paintings are elusive. They seem to invite the viewer to read a narrative, then frustrate the reading. We know from x-rays that details that might have helped unravel a message were later painted out by the artist, as if on second thought he'd chosen a different kind of candor, closer to the complexities of life. His contemporaries held him in high esteem. He enjoyed professional standing and domestic contentment. Then everything came apart.

On May 22, 1672, King Louis XIV of France, the Sun King, led his armies across the Maas River into the United Provinces, as the Netherlands was called. Louis had an appetite for glory and intended to enlarge France to the full extent of what he considered its "natural frontiers." The French army was four times bigger than the Dutch. French soldiers swept through Holland with great savagery. To avoid such horrifying treatment, many Dutch cities and towns capitulated. Whole provinces succumbed to the enemy. Dutch commanders breached the dikes to flood the country in the path of the advancing French, and among the valuable farms swallowed by the invading sea was one belonging to Vermeer's mother-in-law. The family's circumstances collapsed. "As a result," Vermeer's wife, Catharina, would later attest, "and owing to the very great burden of his children, having no means of his own, he had lapsed into such decay and decadence, which he had so taken to heart that, as if he had fallen into a frenzy, in a day and a half had gone from being healthy to being dead." Vermeer was forty-three.

After his death Vermeer's work fell into obscurity until the nineteenth century, when French enthusiasts of Dutch painting rediscovered it, and the small body of pictures began its ascent into the great collections. *Lady Writing a Letter with Her Maid* had shuttled from Delft to Rotterdam to Delft to The Hague. By 1798 it was hanging in the house of either the van Slingenlandt family, in Dordrecht, or Willem Bentinck, in The Hague. Then it vanished for ninety years until the rising appetite for Vermeer pulled it up into the light of day in Vienna, in 1881, when Viktor von Miller zu Aicholz bought it and immediately resold it, for sixty thousand francs, in Paris. The picture bounced around among French dealers and collectors until the first Alfred Beit scooped it up and took it off to London, either in the last years of the nineteenth century or the first of the twentieth. It was in his collection when he died in 1906. It passed to his younger brother, Sir Otto Beit, and in 1930, on Sir Otto's death, to his son, Sir Alfred. And so to Russborough, to Dugdale, to the cottage by the sea, to the Baltimore pier, and back to Russborough again. But luckily, not straight back. First it passed into the hands of the National Gallery of Ireland's keeper of conservation, Andrew O'Connor.

And this produced an unforeseen result.

T HE BEIT PICTURES came to O'Connor because the thieves had manhandled them from their frames, and Sir Alfred wanted the gallery to inspect them. O'Connor was not only well

Andrew O'Connor with Vermeer's Lady Writing a Letter with Her Maid. *(Courtesy of Andrew O'Connor)*

trained but also suited to the task by pedigree. His great-grandfather, also Andrew O'Connor, was a Massachusetts stonemason who had made himself into a sculptor, executing a string of Civil War monuments for towns throughout New England. This sculptor's son, also Andrew, moved to Paris and became a sculptor too. His commissions included the bronze doors of St. Bartholomew's Church on Park Avenue, in midtown Manhattan, and the equestrian statue of General

Under the Overpaint

Lafayette in Washington Square, Baltimore. He was the first non-Frenchman to win a gold medal at the Paris Salon.

The present Andrew O'Connor's father, Patrick, took up the clay in turn. He made a bust of the Irish patriot Robert Emmet, now in the library at Trinity College, Dublin, and another of Commodore John Barry, an Irish native sometimes called the father of the U.S. Navy. He did a portrait of his friend, the boxer Gene Tunney. When art could not support him, he turned to the ring himself, becoming a wrestler and billing himself as "The Heavyweight Champion of Ireland—The Man Who Says He Can Beat Joe Louis!" He had challenged the great boxer to a no-holds-barred fight.

Andrew O'Connor was born in 1943 on Bleecker Street in New York City's Greenwich Village. He completed high school there, dropped out after a year at Columbia University, and joined his father, who had moved to Dublin and set up as a picture dealer and restorer. Finding that he liked repairing paint, Andrew O'Connor went to Rome and enrolled in the Istituto Centrale del Restauro, graduated, and returned to Dublin to a position at the National Gallery. When the Beit pictures were returned from captivity in Cork, O'Connor was given the task of examining them.

The conservation studio is in an airy attic at the top of the gallery's oldest wing. Pictures lean against the wall, and a fine, astringent smell laces the air. A skylight pierces the roof directly above the draftsman's table where O'Connor worked. Usually, O'Connor worked alone, preferring solitude, but this time he had company. Because of Dugdale's connection to the IRA, the police feared an attempt to retake the pictures and had posted a young garda with an Uzi machine pistol in the conservation studio. "He became quite interested in the Vermeer," O'Connor later recalled, "and I became interested in the Uzi. I took a liking to him, and thought it must be boring for him just to sit there, so I offered to get him something to read. He had a sports bag with him, and he leaned down and unzipped it: It was crammed with magazines. 'Ah, sure,' he said, 'I'm used to this kind of thing.'"

On a May morning in 1974 O'Connor swung his magnifying lens out over the Vermeer and began to scrutinize the surface. It looked a bit rough. The maid's shoulder had a scratch; there were two nicks on the chair; a smear of chalk lay smudged across the curtain, probably rubbed from the frame when Dugdale's accomplices had yanked the canvas out. Those would be easy to fix. Two others were much worse.

A cut at the top had sliced right down through the layers of paint almost to the canvas. There was also a deep scratch eleven inches long that had damaged parts of the background, the sleeve of the seated woman, and the carpet that covered the table. The depth of these two abrasions led O'Connor to rule out "localized treatment"—a repair to the varnish. Instead, he would have to remove the entire varnish layer to reach and treat the deeper damage. "The varnish had turned brown and murky anyway," O'Connor said, "and there were some dark places where the surface had been retouched. Frankly, the picture was filthy. I doubt it had been cleaned in a hundred years."

On Friday afternoon, May 10, O'Connor made the first cleaning test on the Vermeer, dabbing a cotton swab into a solution of acetone and swiping lightly at the surface. He chose an edge of the picture where framing would later conceal his experiment. The solution was a mixture of acetone, alcohol, and water. The coat of brittle varnish dissolved, and the paint brightened instantly. O'Connor moved to the left side, dabbing at the darkened curtain. Released from the varnish, the white blazed warmly into life. Confident in his approach, O'Connor told the gallery's director that the picture needed to be completely cleaned and how he wanted to proceed.

Under the Overpaint

On Monday Sir Alfred gave permission to go ahead, although one obstacle remained. The Garda had control of the painting. The damage to it was part of the evidence of a crime, and until the prosecutors had decided how to proceed, the scratches had to stay. They told O'Connor to touch nothing but to safeguard the painting exactly as it was.

In the days that followed, O'Connor had time to think about the picture. Most restorers pass their whole professional lives without having a picture as valuable and rare land on their tables. He had time to wonder about his choice of materials. Acetone, even diluted, is a harsh solvent, and some conservators will not use it under any conditions. "I have it in the cupboard," one restorer told me, "and that's where it stays. The truth is, I'm afraid of it."

"It *is* a harsh solvent," agreed O'Connor, "but I like its volatility. Every compound a restorer uses to remove varnish is potentially dangerous, because they can all remove paint too. On some pictures I'd never use acetone, but the Vermeer was very stable."

A first principle of restoration is never to do something to a picture that cannot later be undone. This is to prevent the permanent alteration of the painted structure of a work according to judgments that subsequent scholarship may reverse. But varnish is not paint. It can easily be put back on when it is taken off. In fact the Beits did want the picture revarnished, this time in a matte finish. O'Connor felt that his attack on the old varnish layer would not disturb Vermeer's paint; oil paint that has had three hundred years to dry is a hardy substance.

Far from backing away, O'Connor increased the potency of the solution and tried it again. The paint stood up. He strengthened the solution three times, closely observing the results until he was satisfied that pure acetone would not harm the paint. His youthfulness—O'Connor was thirty-one years old—may have contributed to his eagerness and tolerance for risk. In the baldest terms, the Vermeer was worth about $150,000 a square inch. When a colleague at the Rijksmuseum in Amsterdam had faced a similar Vermeer restoration (*The Love Letter*, stolen in 1971 and later recovered), an international commission of experts had advised him. O'Connor had O'Connor.

On Monday, May 20, one week after the Beits had given permission, the Garda told him he could start. He waited until the next day, then began. "I guess in the end I was confident enough," he said, "because I just hitched my stool up to the table and started to go at the grime." He used pure acetone.

The varnish dissolved at a touch, and the paint leaped into view. O'Connor moved straight out onto the main area of the painting. Although harsh, acetone volatilizes rapidly, combining with oxygen to become inert. In effect, it vaporizes into nothingness even as its work is done. Because of this, O'Connor felt that the pure solution was the safest, "because it *stopped* working so quickly." Even so, it took some courage; one of the most valuable objects in the Irish state lay in his hands, and he was cleaning it with an acidlike compound.

Restoring such a painting demands intense concentration. Normally, O'Connor would not work on a picture for more than two hours a day, turning to other pictures for a break, then going back and cleaning again, freshened by the interlude. But the Vermeer caught him up, and he poured himself at it through the whole of that Tuesday morning and into the afternoon. Even swept up as he was, O'Connor stopped frequently. He likened the task to driving on a busy freeway, where the prudent driver paces himself with rest stops.

Around four o'clock in the afternoon of May 21, something caught his eye. Exhausted from the concentration, O'Connor was about to quit, when his attention became fixed on a place in the

Under the Overpaint

foreground of the painting, on the floor in front of the woman who is writing. Although he had barely begun to clean it, the Vermeer had been in O'Connor's studio for a month. "By then I knew the picture very well, and I think I was expecting something. It was an area where the paint had been retouched. I was cleaning in that area, and I became intensely aware of a patch of overpaint that was quite recent. I stopped cleaning and took a look through the microscope. Definitely, there was something there."

Overpaint is paint that has been applied by someone altering the original work. By saying it was recent, O'Connor meant it had been applied in the previous one hundred years—at least two hundred years after Vermeer had finished the picture. It was thinly applied and had come off with the varnish as soon as O'Connor had moved into the area.

He concentrated on the spot, and as the overpaint came off, a shape began to establish itself. The color coming out was red. O'Connor immediately thought of sealing wax. "I suppose my first feeling was of confusion, not knowing what it was, but then excitement. I realized quickly it was something interesting. I was concerned about the color—red. In the trade we call red a 'fugitive color,' because it rubs away so easily. If you use the wrong cleaner, it can come right off. You have to act with particular care. I stopped and went home. I'm not really much of a worrier, and I wasn't nervous or overly concerned; just excited."

O'Connor labored at the area all the next day and into the following day. He kept his disciplined approach, cleaning steadily and carefully, always alert to the relative flightiness of the pigment he was uncovering. At his elbow stood a pair of little bottles, one with the acetone and another containing white spirit, a petroleum distillate. A quick dab of white spirit would immediately halt the dissolving action of a cleaning solvent. It was unlikely O'Connor would need it, because the acetone stopped working quickly anyway. But the white spirit was a standard insurance policy of the restorer's craft, and O'Connor was too careful not to have it on hand.

Once he focused exclusively on the red pigment, the uncovering went quickly. The dot of red grew into a symmetrical shape, until finally there it lay, a small patch of crimson glowing on the tiles of Vermeer's room. This was a breathtaking moment, and O'Connor laid the cotton swab aside and studied the little image. Finally, he was certain about it. His first intuition had been right: It was a depiction of a red wax seal. His head buzzing with speculations about what the discovery might mean, he hurried downstairs to tell the director, James White.

White was not a professional art historian but was well known in Dublin for his love affair with art. He was seated at his desk when his young restorer barged in with the news of his discovery. White listened intently as O'Connor spilled out what he had found. "I don't think he realized at first what I was going on about," O'Connor remembered, "but then it sunk in and he got up immediately and followed me back upstairs."

From a painter as spare with information as Vermeer, any extra detail, as White had realized, would say something crucial about the scene. In Dutch society of the seventeenth century, paper was a precious commodity and a letter an important object. That this one lay scrunched and discarded on the floor had already suggested haste. The seal, scattered on the floor nearby, raised the level of emotion in the painting. The seated woman had torn the letter open with enough abandon to dislodge the wax and send the seal skittering onto the tiles.

White returned to his office and immediately telephoned the Beits. O'Connor was invited to write an account of his discovery for the prestigious London art journal *Burlington Magazine*. As scholars read the painting now, they see a woman who has received a letter

Under the Overpaint

from her lover, possibly breaking off the affair, and in a controlled frenzy she is dashing off a reply. The maid knows everything.

T HE PICTURE THAT RETURNED to Russborough brought this new narrative along, and of course it brought another too. It brought the tale of its own theft. The Vermeer was no longer simply art but, to those who knew its story, loot.

{ 4 }

The General

A T THE TIME THE VERMEER joined the rest of the collection at Russborough, a twenty-four-year-old Dubliner named Martin Cahill was just beginning to establish himself as a serious criminal. He was a rotund and crafty serpent whose passions included pigeons, curries, and cake. He spoke in a soft, northside brogue. Often he wore a balaclava pulled over his head, and to mock police when about to confront them, a Mickey Mouse T-shirt. He neither smoked nor drank, but loved to visit pubs; he drank orange soda. Once, he stapled a man's fingers to the floor, one by one, then drove nails through his victim's palms, in an attempt to extract information. When Cahill realized the man did not possess the information, he apologized. He never took a holiday, never stepped out of Ireland in his life, had no passport. He disliked foreigners. He had six motorcycles, including a Harley-Davidson, and owned none of them. If he had, the ownership might have come between him and his welfare check.

He was slovenly, loyal, suspicious, immovable. Once, on his way to court, he robbed a branch of the Allied Irish Bank on Richmond Street in central Dublin. "It was his favorite bank," a Dublin crime writer said, "because it was a block from the Garda social club. He

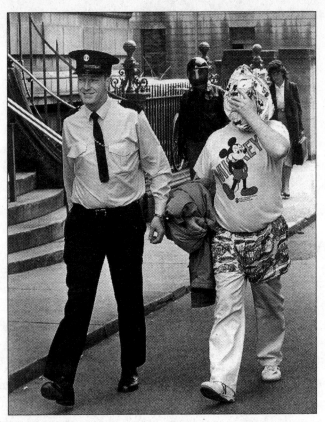

Martin Cahill under arrest in July 1988, wearing a Mickey Mouse shirt and covering his face. (Irish Times)

hated the Guards, and liked to rub their faces in it if he could." He hit the bank at 10:55 a.m., handed the money to an accomplice, and presented himself at the Central Criminal Court exactly eight minutes later, on time for a remand hearing.

"Ah, sure, he was a son of a bitch," a Dublin detective told me in an exasperated voice. "He stank that much you wouldn't want to breathe when you were near him."

And for the time he reigned, there was not an object safe in Dublin . . . or in County Wicklow.

MARTIN JOSEPH CAHILL was born in 1949 in a hellish slum north of the Liffey. He was the second of Agnes Cahill's twelve surviving children. His father, Patrick, was a laborer who became a Dublin lighthouse keeper and a drunk. In James Joyce's story *A Little Cloud*, the protagonist walks down Henrietta Street, a thoroughfare not far from where the Cahills lived on Grenville Street. "They stood or ran in the doorway," Joyce wrote of the urchins Cahill would have recognized, "or crawled up the steps before the gaping doors or squatted like mice upon the thresholds. . . . He picked his way deftly through all that minute vermin-like life and under the shadow of the gaunt spectral mansions in which the old nobility of Dublin had roistered."

Martin Cahill made his first appearance in the courts at the age of twelve, was convicted of larceny and let off with a warning. Two years later he was back on the same charge and fined a pound. Two months after that he was back again, for larceny and housebreaking. This time he was sentenced to two years in St. Conleth's reformatory in Daingean, County Offaly, an institution staffed by priests and brothers of the Oblates of Mary Immaculate. The regime was strict, and boys who broke the rules were paraded out in their pajamas at nightfall, to the front steps of the dormitory, where they bent over and received their punishment from a proctor wielding a two-foot strap.

At St. Conleth's Cahill conceived his trademark stance in the face of authority—ignore it. He avoided eye contact with his warders at all times. If he didn't look at them, he reasoned, he didn't have to say "hello." He didn't have to say "father" or "brother." He reduced the chance that they would speak to *him*.

According to Cahill, this system for avoiding trouble failed him only once. He was walking down a corridor when some brother came surging along in a private fury. Cahill, as usual, kept his eyes on the floor. Suddenly, just as they were abreast, the cleric seized Cahill and gave him three hard clouts on the jaw. "Stop sniggering!" he bellowed, and stamped away.

Cahill returned from St. Conleth's to find that his parents, unable or unwilling to pay rent, had been moved from one public-housing project to another in a steady decline, until at last they'd landed in a ramshackle, pestilential slum called Hollyfield Buildings. This noxious tenement, in the Rathmines quarter, was the city of Dublin's dumping ground for its most intractable charges. Cahill loved it, finding in the impoverished community a bond whose principal cement was an instinctive hatred of police.

In 1968, at the age of nineteen, Cahill met and married Frances Lawless, a shy girl whose family also lived in Hollyfield. He seems to have made an effort to go straight. More or less illiterate even after two years at St. Conleth's, he took a laboring job in a noisome, dust-choked factory making cardboard boxes. The job ran out when orders for the boxes dwindled. He found another position, this time making sacks. The plant ran night and day, churning out its product in a din set up by ancient, bone-weary machines that had to be coaxed along from hour to hour by a crew of exhausted, stone-deaf artificers. Cahill said his head had felt as if it would explode. One morning after a twelve-hour shift, with a thin, brown string of dried blood running from his ear to his chin, Cahill walked out of the place for the last time. He hated it; his wife was pregnant; they needed extra money. He fell in with a scheme to rob a warehouse full of cigarettes. "I'll be back in a few minutes," he said to Frances; but he did not return. He was caught in a police trap, and in 1970 was sentenced to four years in Mountjoy prison.

Cahill said later that at Mountjoy he had learned to read. He took Dale Carnegie correspondence courses in self-improvement and devoured the book *How to Win Friends and Influence People.* He relished the solitude of his cell, saying, "It gave me time to think. One way or another you have to do your time. You can fight it in your head or use it to do something positive."

Much has been written about Cahill. Some have called him "cunning" or "implacable," or labeled him a "mastermind" who conducted an "unrelenting war of wits" with the Garda. The fact that he bothered to think about such things as how to get away after a robbery is displayed as proof of his malevolent genius. I think the evidence supports a simpler claim, that he was meticulous, and certainly suspicious, and that in his cell at Mountjoy these attributes got welded into something useful to him, like a principle.

He hated the police, in particular a Garda detective inspector named Ned Ryan. A Dublin magazine wrote of Ryan that "he looks and sounds like a slightly lisping but lugubrious Edward G. Robinson: pudgy, balding, heavy-lidded and jug-eared." When Cahill got out of Mountjoy in 1973, Ryan pulled him in to grill him about a robbery, and finished the interview by promising to squash him like a bug. "You're going to be reduced to robbing grannies' handbags," he told Cahill. Cahill said nothing and did not look at Ryan, and although in the years ahead the Garda certainly squeezed Cahill, it was Ryan, and not Cahill, who needed round-the-clock protection when he learned that a contract had been put out on his life. There was to be no handbag stealing for Cahill.

After Mountjoy, Cahill found his way back into the Dublin demimonde. For a short period he consorted with the gangster Henry Dunne. Then, in 1974, less than a year after his release from prison, and dissatisfied with the way Dunne divided loot, Cahill

The General

formed a gang of his own and promptly attacked an armored truck collecting the day's receipts from Quinnsworth's, a department store in Dublin's Rathfarnham district. The gang struck a guard on the head and escaped with ninety-two thousand pounds, a huge haul at the time. Within a day the police learned Cahill was the robber, and raided Hollyfield Buildings, arresting him and his brother, Eddie, and another of his men. They shoved them into a van and took them down to the Bridewell Garda station.

Later, the police told Cahill that one of his associates had confessed. Cahill said nothing. He didn't look at them; he answered not the slightest question. This was the first taste for the gardaí of Cahill's rule of behavior when in custody: act as if your captors don't exist. More than simple animosity fueled this behavior. In the long hours in his cell at Mountjoy, Cahill had decided that there was no such thing as harmless information in a conversation with police. In a series of interviews in 1988 with Michael O'Higgins, then a journalist and later a leading Dublin barrister, Cahill spelled out the rationale behind his inflexible silence. Gardaí, he maintained, are never just talking. Idle chat about the weather may progress, quite naturally, to trivial-seeming talk about their families and then about yours. According to Cahill, the small personal details gathered by gardaí, which they could not have known without the accused's cooperation, lent credence to other evidence, sometimes fabricated.

In the Bridewell after the Quinnsworth's hit, Cahill sat on a chair in the hall for two straight days, saying not a word. Finally, the gardaí charged him and threw him into a cell with a stray dog, apparently in the hope that the animal would irritate Cahill. He later claimed to have lain down beside the dog and gone to sleep. The next day, in Rathfarnham District Court, the charge against him was thrown out for lack of evidence. He went back to Hollyfield Buildings and moved his brand-new Harley-Davidson motor-cycle out into plain view in front of the slum, so the gardaí tailing him could not fail to miss it.

Cahill and the gardaí settled into mutual loathing. They recognized early in Cahill's career that he was a leader. It is not in the nature of police to admire this quality in criminals, but they took it seriously. At every opportunity they harassed him. The bitterness between them grew. In Cahill, the antagonism fed a natural capacity for patience, and in his world his reputation flourished.

I N THE DUBLIN CRIME PRESS, the need to cover Cahill's blossoming career without committing libel led to the use of an alias: the General. Whoever coined this moniker got it exactly right, for Cahill's strength lay in his ability to organize essentially untruthful, violent braggarts—the raw recruits of crime—into orderly platoons. That he could do this, and deserved to be called the General, was irrefutably established on a sunny morning in late July 1983, when Cahill assaulted a Dublin treasure-house.

Thomas O'Connor and Sons, jewelry manufacturers, had a plant in the Dublin quarter of Harold's Cross. Six million dollars' worth of gold and gems lay inside. Not surprisingly, others had already thought of stealing these jewels. The IRA had formed a plan, then dropped it, deciding they could not dismantle the alarms, which were connected by dedicated line to a Garda quick-response unit at Dublin Castle. In 1982 Henry Dunne had begun to plan an attack on the factory with men disguised as gardaí, but ended up in jail for something else before he could pull it off. Cahill stepped into the breach.

On July 26 at 9 p.m. the conspirators met at a pub in Milltown called the Dropping Well. They posed as a team of soccer friends relaxing after a match. They wore grass-stained clothes and laughed and drank and talked loudly about the game. Each had a large sports bag, ostensibly stuffed with equipment—as indeed it was. But the equipment was automatic pistols, percussion grenades, stun guns, smoke bombs, balaclavas, radios, and, because Cahill thought of everything, gloves.

At 1 a.m. they left the pub, climbed into a waiting van, and drove to a street alongside the O'Connor factory. A central courtyard was enclosed by the factory on two sides, and a high wall surrounded the rest. Three men got over the wall and forced open the door to the boiler room, an area not guarded by alarms. The others dispersed to pick up stolen cars.

At 7:55 a.m. Robert Kinlan, a plant manager, arrived to unlock the gates. This deactivated the alarms. The next to arrive was the general manager, Daniel Fitzgibbon, who drove through the entrance at precisely 8 a.m. Fitzgibbon went in and opened the safe, and at 8:02 the bandits swooped into the courtyard in their stolen cars and seized the factory. Arriving staff were grabbed at the gate and hustled into the toilets, along with Kinlan and Fitzgibbon. Cahill cleaned the place out in thirty-five minutes, sending a cascade of big, black headlines into the Irish press and sealing his place in the front rank of Dublin gangsters.

CAHILL LOST MOST OF the O'Connor haul. He had a plan to transfer the loot to England in the doors of a car, but someone broke into the cache while the vehicle was on the ferry, and cleaned it out. Cahill suspected the courier, who was so frightened he didn't come home for a week, and that was the gentleman who ended up stapled to the floor.

Other operations must have produced a better return, because when he left Hollyfield Buildings (the city demolished the slum) he was able to buy his two-story, fully detached, middle-class house in Cowper Downs with a bank draft for eighty-five thousand pounds. He put it in his sister-in-law's name. It sat in a row of identical, sand-colored brick dwellings arrayed around a square. Each house had a low wall and a garden in the front. Today they are million-dollar houses. "He lived like a pig inside," a Dublin detective said. "He didn't care what kind of house he had; he only moved there to thumb his nose at us."

His personal life was complicated by de facto bigamy. He consorted openly with his wife's sister, Tina Lawless. Cahill cared nothing for the forms of civic respectability but could display a lively sense of the values of the community. When the drug trade came to Dublin, a group called Concerned Parents Against Drugs formed to confront the peddlers. Seeing a way to score publicity points, Cahill created his own organization, Ordinary Decent Criminals, and sent men out with placards lettered *ODC* to support the parents. The men were reluctant. Cahill ordered them out anyway, and they went. He was a tubby little troll, with his thinning hair and pasty skin and bargain-basement clothes, but he would have broken their arms and tossed them in the river if they'd blinked at his orders.

Cahill loved a robbery. It added to his pleasure if the task was difficult and the accomplishment could be read as an affront to the police. To develop the tactics for such crimes was pure delight, and he guarded his plans from everyone. Even his close associates he kept at bay. He had a fear of people "getting religion" at some future time and betraying him. He seems to have learned to love aloneness at Mountjoy, and to have used that gift to think and think and think about his crimes. His appetite for detail was legendary, and so when a criminal named Paddy Shanahan thought of a job that would dwarf every other caper in the history of Ireland, he brought it to Cahill.

Outwardly, Shanahan looked like the prosperous businessman that he once had been. He'd had success as an auctioneer and builder in Kildare but had been hopelessly seduced by the frisson of crime. Shanahan loved the act of pulling on a balaclava; guns delighted him. For ten years he ran a sideline stealing mailbags from the Kildare train. He once helped the Dunne gang plot a warehouse raid that scored one hundred thousand pounds' worth of cigarettes. The Garda had never caught him, but the English did, sending him to prison for the 1981 robbery of a Staffordshire antiques collector. The victim, seventy-two years old, had collapsed from a heart attack when Shanahan burst in. Shanahan did four years, and when he came home to Ireland in 1985, had only one thing on his mind: what to steal next.

He found a target with much to recommend it. The location was remote. Dozens of escape routes led away from the vicinity into wild country. The site was poorly protected. Best of all, the place was a treasure trove. In the length and breadth of Ireland there was nothing like it. It had been assaulted only once before: by amateurs. Of course, the target was Russborough.

In Dublin they say that Shanahan made a dossier to take to Cahill, with maps and a plan of the house and a list of its contents. He hoped to appeal to the General's fondness for tactics by presenting him with the layout, like a battlefield for toy soldiers, something for the plotter to seize on right away. Cahill did seize on it. Apparently, the challenge swept him up. The job would be the biggest sack in modern Ireland. Cahill told Shanahan he would get back to him, which he did not, because he didn't trust him. Instead he took the target for himself.

On his Kawasaki (the Harley-Davidson was too well known), Cahill rode out of Dublin and up into the Wicklow Mountains.

He felt safe up there. No one could have followed him without being seen; the vistas run for miles. He probably went up to the Sally Gap, a crossroads high up on top, then picked his way down toward Blessington. There are good views from Mullaghcleevaun, a hill he could have climbed with the Kawasaki. The summit is almost three thousand feet; Russborough lies down below in the green valley.

Cahill knew the mountains well. He had hidden things there. He is said to have buried a stash of silver so well that he could not find it again, and spent weekends digging fruitlessly. Murdered gangsters are buried there too, and the phrase "a trip to the mountains" has the same meaning in Dublin as "cement overshoes" in New York. A driver in the hills often comes upon some burned-out wreck, destroyed after use in a crime. Cahill rode around up there, then down into the valley and across the N81 and up behind Russborough, through villages like Brannockstown and Ballymore Eustace, and out as far as Naas, on the highway to Limerick. He studied the vicinity until the map of it was printed in his head.

Next he built a bunker to hide the goods. In a forested place Cahill and two confederates dug a pit six feet deep and five feet wide, lined it with concrete blocks, and covered the blocks with plastic sheets. They put a plank roof over it, covered it with dirt, and camouflaged the pit with pine needles and clumps of peat. The entrance was sealed with a steel manhole cover and camouflaged as well. This was in February 1986.

The Beits had begun to open their house to the public from Easter to November. Easter fell at the end of March that year, and Cahill waited until the following Sunday, April 6, then went out alone, paid the one-pound admission, and trailed around with the rest of the visitors. No doubt he paid attention to the location of the pictures. He also must have looked for the alarms, and to see how the doors were fastened, and what it looked like out back and up the hill behind the house. He went out again the next Sunday, again alone. After that, for the next three Sundays in a row, he took accomplices along.

Some of the men who went to Russborough thought they should ignore the pictures. High-value art was notoriously hard to fence. They favored taking antiques, such as porcelain and clocks, the kind of items they had stolen before and knew how to sell. Cahill would not be swayed. He wanted the pictures, and he knew he must act soon. According to his biography, Cahill had discovered that Paddy Shanahan, concluding that Cahill had no intention of including him, had decided to raid the house himself. Shanahan had already hired a London criminal who specialized in alarms. This man, so Cahill learned, was about to leave for Dublin. Cahill moved.

ON THE NIGHT OF May 17, a Saturday, the gang fanned out into Dublin and stole two jeeps and three cars, and fitted them with false license plates. Cahill assembled the last recruits. There were sixteen in all: drivers, men for the alarms, mechanics, and blaggers. "Blaggers are the lads with the heavy metal," a Dublin crime reporter explained. "In a bank robbery, it's the blaggers who convince people not to go ringing alarms."

Some of these men knew the target, and others did not. One man's job, for example, was to drive a stolen black Citroën out the N7 to Naas and abandon it there, to confuse police later. The others went out of Dublin by different routes, some of them going down the seashore to Bray and cutting up into the mountains. The meeting time was set for midnight, May 21, near the Sally Gap.

Up there, Cahill gave the last instructions. Some drivers went off to wait at various rendezvous. Cahill drove down in a jeep and took the Ballymore Eustace road that leads along the stone bound-

Russborough, just visible through the trees. Cahill and his gang approached through these woods and across the pasture on the night they robbed the Beits. (Matthew Hart)

ary wall on the north side of the estate, above and behind the house. A gate for farm vehicles pierces the wall, and that's where they went in. They came down through a stand of beech and oak. Cahill planted wire stakes and flagged the route with strips of white plastic torn from shopping bags, marking the way for the jeep to return when they were through. A quarter mile from the house the woods gave way to pasture. The robbers made their way through a herd of cows and flagged the pasture too. They crossed the fence that separated the meadow from the lawn. All the windows on that side of the mansion were dark; the house was fast asleep. At 2:20 a.m. the raiders reached the broad steps of the north front. They stole up and cut a small rectangle out of a pane of glass in the French doors. Cahill reached inside and forced the shutters open. He stepped through into the house, activating the infrared motion detector. The alarm began to ring. This set the stage for one of the strangest sequences in crime, for whatever Cahill had

The General

then planned to do, what with the alarm bells ringing, he soon found himself facing a development he had not foreseen: A car with two policemen was a mile from the house.

As Cahill knew and had relied on, the tiny Garda detachment at Blessington was closed at night. The Russborough alarm, normally routed to Blessington, would have gone instead to Naas. Naas would pass the alert to Baltinglass, a divisional headquarters twenty miles from Russborough. And that's exactly how it went, except that at that very moment two gardaí from Baltinglass, having just dropped off a package of documents at the Blessington Garda post, were returning home along the N81, practically in front of Russborough.

"We'd just passed the house when the call came through," Jim Lawlor later recalled. "We made a U-turn and went back fast. You couldn't see anything wrong from the road. The front of the house was all lit up, which was normal." They came to the Russborough turn and took the corner hard. This brought them into the narrow road that runs along the high stone fence and is hidden from the house. They had their lights out anyway. They reached the main gates, swung through, and came rapidly up the drive. As the house came into view, the two gardaí would have been looking along the illuminated length of the facade. The kitchen wing would have screened the back of the house and the fields that rise above it. The gardaí could see nothing of the men who were there, or their flagged route up the hill. Then suddenly a man stepped into view, coming from the far end of the house and into the brilliant illumination of the front.

Under the circumstances, he was a suspect. Lawlor pulled the car in front of him, got out, and asked him who he was. He was a boyfriend of one of the maids, and he'd just walked her home. "It was plain he was telling the truth," said Lawlor, "and we went straight to that end of the house, and into the side courtyard and knocked on the door. The girl was still right by the door, and she let us in. She thought it was her boyfriend coming back. So we were in there pretty quick. I told her we were responding to an alarm, and she went and got the chauffeur."

The Beits were in London. The chauffeur, Tom Brosnan, led Lawlor and his partner into the main part of the house, then went to get the Russborough administrator, Lieutenant-Colonel Michael O'Shea, a retired army officer. A few minutes later O'Shea arrived, in dressing gown and slippers. Lawlor asked to see the alarm control-box. O'Shea took the gardaí down a long corridor. They found the box, and Lawlor opened it. "I could see the alarm was showing for a section of the house, and I asked him to reset the alarm. He reset it, and it rang again. I asked him to take me to the section shown, to check it, but he said no, for me to wait, and he'd check it himself. I asked him if he was happy with that, and he said he was."

O'Shea came back and told them that nothing was amiss, and they could leave. They did.

Years later I put these facts to Chief Superintendent Feely when we met at the Downshire Hotel in Blessington, because he had still been at the Blessington detachment when the events occurred. He drew a deep breath and sank back in his chair and crossed his legs. "Well, now, that alarm," he said, "that alarm had been a sensor-type alarm. It sent a beam around the room, and if it was interrupted, the alarm went off. But you could fool it. Let's say you hung a little box in front of the alarm before it was turned back on. The beam could then move around inside the little box, so its pattern wouldn't be broken."

"And did you find a little box?"

"No," he conceded, "that little box—that could never be proved."

Feely sat for a moment, casting his mind back over the events.

"He was a hardy bit of stuff," he said, meaning O'Shea. "He was very angry. He was a lieutenant colonel. He had a gun up there, and I've no doubt at all he would have shot them if he'd come on them."

Anyway, he did not come on them, and lucky for him, because they were standing out there with Kalashnikov assault rifles. I wanted to make sure I understood the sequence of events, and being unable to locate O'Shea, I called Jim Lawlor and drove out to Baltinglass to see him. Baltinglass is a pretty town with a ruined abbey and a humped, stone bridge across the Liffey. Lawlor is still a garda there. It was a Saturday, and his shift ended at 2:00 p.m., and he joined me a few minutes after that in the dining room of Quinn's Hotel. Lawlor is a slim, young-looking man in his forties with thick dark hair and blue eyes. A native Dubliner, he had always wanted to live in the country and had jumped at the chance of a posting to Baltinglass. He had been on the force ten years when he answered the Russborough alarm. We reviewed the events of the night.

"And I guess Cahill was, what, twenty feet away, standing outside in the dark?"

"Or maybe inside, behind a curtain," Lawlor replied.

"Do you think about that?"

Lawlor stubbed out a cigarette and smiled. "Sure I think about it. Why didn't I insist? I think about it all the time."

We sat in silence for a minute. It was cold outside, and the busy warmth of the dining room, with the clatter of plates and the cheerful noise of talk, was welcome. I took one of Lawlor's cigarettes, and we finished our coffee. Finally, I said, "Did anything happen later?"

Lawlor shook his head. "I resumed patrol. The rest of the night was uneventful."

But not at Russborough. At Russborough the thieves swept

through the mansion. They took eighteen paintings, including two by Rubens, a Goya, a Gainsborough, two Metsus, and the most valuable picture on any wall in Ireland: Vermeer's *Lady Writing a Letter with Her Maid*. Six minutes later they melted away back up the hill and into the sleeping countryside of County Wicklow.

{ 5 }

Stalking Cahill

CAHILL DROVE TEN MILES to Manor Kilbride and, for reasons still unknown, jettisoned seven paintings in the grass. Perhaps, in the midst of dividing the haul into smaller lots for concealment, an approaching car surprised them. Or Cahill may have wanted to register his contempt for the art, as a warning to police not to expect, in any subsequent dealing, special treatment for the paintings. The thieves flung the discarded pictures near the shore of Blessington Lake and dispersed into the mountains. Cahill and two others drove to the bunker, secreted the remaining eleven paintings, and went back down to Dublin. As he came from the hills into his native city, with the night's work behind him and the light of dawn seeping into the sky, Cahill was elated. Witnesses said he could hardly keep still in the car.

Suddenly, a Garda patrol car happened upon them as they came down the Terenure Road. One of the gardaí recognized Cahill and swung the car around and tore up behind him with blue lights flashing. As a known criminal, Cahill could be searched at will under various pretexts. The mood in Cahill's car evaporated. They had ditched their weapons, but muddy gloves lay on the floor and mud thickly caked their boots from the trek down through the field and their work at the pit where the paintings were hidden. As they pulled over, Cahill hissed at the others that the police could know nothing, and that the interception posed no real threat to them. It was not a crime in Ireland to be dirty.

Then he leaped from the car and began to strip off his clothes, screaming: "I don't want to talk to youse. I'm being harassed by police." The officers searched the car anyway, ignoring Cahill as well as they could while he pranced and shouted in the road. They couldn't have missed the gloves and the clotted mud on the floor. They must have been a little rattled by Cahill raging around in the road as though demented; they got back in their car and drove away. Cahill went directly to Rathmines Garda station and marched up to an astonished duty sergeant and lodged a complaint of police harassment, making him write it down and note the time. Some observers claim that Cahill took these steps to prepare the basis for an alibi, but this cannot be true. Evidence that the country's top gangster had been stopped at dawn in Dublin several hours after a robbery in Wicklow would establish, not that he couldn't have done it, but that he probably had. A more convincing explanation would be that, since he had been caught out in inconvenient circumstances, he might as well thumb his nose at the Garda. Half an hour later he strolled out of the Rathmines station, a thief at the top of his game, with the biggest heist in Ireland hours behind him and the loot buried in the Wicklow hills.

Cahill was not returning to his old life, though. He had crossed an invisible line that night. Nothing would ever be the same for him again.

IN WICKLOW the cry went up at nine o'clock. One pictures Colonel O'Shea, having tossed and turned after being roused from his sleep in the middle of the night, finally getting up and cinching his dressing gown back into place and heading downstairs for another look at the room where there had been that business of the alarm. Of course, he noticed that the walls were bare. There were tire tracks outside in the meadow, and bits of plastic fluttering from stakes, and within two hours the place was crawling with crime-scene gardaí from Phoenix Park. The press came busting down the road from Blessington. Sir Alfred, hounded by reporters at his London home, stepped out and said: "I cannot think other than that one of these sort of revolutionary movements are behind the theft and are seeking a ransom which they won't get. It is not me that has been robbed this time— it is the Irish people, since the collection is now in trust for the state."

So the news, secret until that moment, was out. Sir Alfred and Lady Beit had spent almost a year negotiating the terms of a magnificent gift to the National Gallery of Ireland. The gift included the Vermeer and the Goya. This splendid benefaction had been weeks away from moving down the N81 to Dublin; the pictures robbed from Russborough in effect belonged to Ireland.

At first the police believed the hit on Russborough had been a foreign operation, by an international gang with a ready overseas market. They feared the pictures might already have left Ireland in a private plane. One of their reasons for positing an out-of-country origin for the crime was that the usual pool of police informants had dried up like the Sahara. In the immediate aftermath of the crime, the Garda could not find a single lead. The paintings had gone off into the Irish night without so much as a ripple to show where. They were works of such stature that it seemed only natural to suppose their theft was the work of some sophisticated syndicate, crooks with banking and auction-house connections, and surely not just a bunch of thugs from Dublin with a jeep.

This thinking did not prevail long. The sheer dearth of information suggested a different conclusion: It *was* a bunch of thugs from Dublin, but with an extraordinarily tight control of the underworld. The city's "snouts," as the Irish call informants, were obviously afraid. There was only one criminal able to summon such fear: Cahill. And as police already knew, he had been out that night.

For a while, no leads seeped out of the silence; but in time they did. The Garda started to hear whispers about Russborough, and the Wicklow Mountains, and Cahill. Some of their deepest sources inside the criminal hierarchy—"moles," they call them—fed out scraps of information. This information was beginning to circulate for the simple reason that the General's next task necessarily took him outside his own circle and into a realm where his writ did not run. That task was unloading the booty.

The challenge of disposing of stolen art introduces the novice art thief to the snag that lies beneath the smooth surface of the crime: Art is easy to steal but hard to sell. This is particularly true of works by famous artists. Scholarly catalogues raisonnés—complete inventories of the artist's work, with a detailed history of the ownership of each item—make it impossible to sell such works into the legitimate trade. The true art thief will ignore a Rembrandt or Vermeer or Goya and take instead a work by a lesser master, for which there is a market but not a large body of documentary evidence chronicling ownership. An eighteenth-century flower painting by Pieter Casteels III, for example, would be worth some one hundred thousand dollars, less than a thousandth of the price of a Vermeer. On the other hand, a criminal may easily sell it into the legitimate trade, because the purchaser can maintain that he did not know it was stolen, even if he suspects it was. If the thief pockets seven thousand dollars (7 percent of market value is about what the robber will get), it is not bad for a night's work.

Cahill faced a challenge of a different order of magnitude. There would be no 7 percent from the neighborhood art store. Next to the Nazis' looting of Jewish art collections in World War II, Rose Dugdale's robbery had been the greatest art theft in history. Cahill's had now replaced it. He had fewer pictures than Dugdale, but a rising market had pushed their value to about one hundred million dollars. To unload this haul, Cahill would need to turn outward, from the closed circle he had lived in all his life to the wider world. He would need to seek out criminals with an appetite for what he had. This need forced Cahill into an arena prowled by adversaries he was not used to. One of them was Scotland Yard. The famous police force had long experience with art thieves, and an active intelligence network. It also had a plentiful supply of undercover operatives, including a large and crafty package of bonhomie named Charley Hill.

N O FORCE in the world of art crime exactly equals Hill, an enormous, polished man with a football player's build and a round, chubby face and shrewd brown eyes that seem always to be probing. It was Hill who in 2002, as a private detective, recovered the marquess of Bath's twenty-million-pound Titian, *Rest on the Flight into Egypt*. When I asked a London insurance operative who'd been close to the case how much Hill had made, he gave me a wintry smile and said, "I daresay he covered his expenses."

On a January day in 2002, as a hurricane blew itself out over southeastern England, I took the London underground from Green Park to a suburban destination south of the River Thames to meet the detective. Ragged clouds went scudding above the trees as Hill came down the high street in a tiny Peugeot, made a U-turn in front of the station, and squeaked to a stop. He wore an amazingly orange tweed jacket, a tattersall shirt, and old, wrecked corduroy pants. He looked and sounded 100 percent English. But Charley Hill is not 100 percent anything.

He was born in Britain, the son of an American air force officer and an English mother. His early boyhood was spent at his maternal grandfather's rural English vicarage. He moved to the United States in time for high school, where, according to one account, he was a classmate of "a young wannabe journalist called Al Gore." Hill fought in Vietnam, was cited for valor, and went to read history at Trinity College, Dublin. He left Trinity before graduating, moved to London, studied theology, and joined Scotland Yard. He became a devout churchman (he took me to see his parish church) and a devoted cop. He lives on a leafy street of redbrick Victorian townhouses with gleaming doors and polished handles and gardens imprisoned by black-metal fences. Inside Hill's house is a faded pink sofa, bookshelves sagging with art books, and some prints hanging crookedly on the walls.

Hill is a man with a well-stocked cupboard of identities: Anglican, policeman, art lover, Englishman, American. From these he is able to take what he needs, and wear it convincingly at will. In undercover work, such a person is the pot of gold.

Hill's first contact with the Irish criminals came the year before the Russborough job. In 1985 Scotland Yard's Regional Crime squad put Hill in touch with Tommy Coyle, a legendary Irish fence who was putting out the word that he might soon have art to sell. British police had once caught Coyle boarding a flight to Dublin with £77.3 million in treasury bonds in his luggage—allegedly his share of a £291-million robbery of a London courier company. Coyle beat the charge and lived in ample comfort in the Irish countryside. He owned a racehorse named 77 Mill, in honor of the treasury bonds. Informants now told the Yard that Coyle had surfaced again and was looking for art buyers. This intelligence was passed to the Art and Antiques squad, which decided to put in Hill.

Stalking Cahill

Because of Hill's American background, he favored cover identities that called for an American accent. The alias he chose was Charley Berman. Hill liked the name because it had two *r*s—a letter pronounced differently in North America than in Britain. The ability to toss off American *r*s, Hill had found, made him credible as an American. Berman's identity was that of an American crook with an interest in art. His phone number was leaked to Coyle, and Coyle called him. "We got on fine," said Hill. "He told me there was going to be a series of big jobs. He said, 'We're going to build up an Aladdin's cave!'"

Hill described Coyle as "very cautious, very canny—a likable rogue." He began to call Hill often, promising "things" soon to be on offer. This went on through the last months of 1985 and into the next year until, on the evening of May 21, 1986, Coyle called Hill and said that something big was going down that night, and Hill would read about it in the papers. Hill did, for that was the night Cahill robbed Russborough. The next day Coyle called.

"Well, there you go," he said in a merry voice, "didn't I tell you?"

"You bet," said Hill.

"Do you think you'd like to see them articles?"

"Darn right."

But before Hill could arrange to see the Russborough pictures, a complication developed, one that threatened to wreck his cover. Coyle announced to Hill that a Renoir would soon be on offer. Hill said that was very nice, and asked the Irishman to call him once he had it. The problem was that Hill knew there had been no Renoir at Russborough. From what Coyle had said, there was only one Renoir he could have meant: *The Girl with the Watering Can*. The painting was part of the collection of the late Sir Hugh Lane, an Irish picture dealer who'd gone down on the *Lusitania*. Under the terms of his will, the painting shuttled back and forth between the National Gallery in London and the Dublin municipal gallery. At the time of Coyle's call, it was in Dublin. Coyle's associates meant to steal it, in an assault in the heart of Dublin. There was only one criminal in Dublin in 1985 audacious enough for the attempt: Martin Cahill.

Hill's quandary lay in the possibility that if he tipped the Irish police, and security at the museum suddenly increased, Coyle might conclude that Hill, as Charley Berman, had betrayed him. Hill and his superiors at Scotland Yard felt they had no choice. "The Lane collection was not well protected. Cahill could have emptied the place. So we warned the Garda, and they put on more security and Cahill spotted it, as we knew he would, and called off the robbery."

At first it looked as if Hill's fears had been prescient, because Coyle stopped calling. Everything went quiet. Cahill had gone to ground. The Russborough pictures stayed in a hole in the Wicklow Mountains. Three months passed without a word. Then Coyle called Hill again, as jolly as before, and said they were ready to deal.

Hill and Coyle had not met face-to-face. They had spoken only by phone. To get to the point of actually entering the same room and looking each other in the eye, they would follow the protocols designed by criminals to keep themselves from being caught by men like Hill. The basic procedural element is a check on identity. Hill made an elaborate pretense of demanding criminal references from Coyle. To satisfy Coyle's own demands, the Garda supplied a turned Irish crook and Scotland Yard provided a well-known English criminal figure—in fact, a policeman under cover—to vouch for Hill. Coyle accepted the bona fides. In August of 1986 he flew to London and met Hill in a room that "Charley Berman" had taken at the Post House Hotel near Heathrow airport.

"He came in the morning," Hill later recalled. "He was a short, dark-haired Irishman, loads of chat, a great talker, tweed jacket, open-necked shirt. I had on khaki pants, like a real American. We

Stalking Cahill

talked about the paintings, and I said, 'There's going to be all kinds of problems, because this is the biggest theft since the last time they were stolen.' I was trying to cool things off, to relax them and slow them down. They were all keyed up. I wanted to get them hooked, and I thought the best way was to be noncommittal. We had breakfast in my room. He headed off back to Ireland convinced I was the best guy to do business with."

Among police, optimism rose. Hill and Coyle had hit it off. Coyle obviously had Cahill's trust. The operation was progressing well, when all at once it fell apart. The Irish criminal who'd turned double agent died of a drug overdose. This threatened a key link between Coyle and Hill, because it had been the Irishman who had vouched for Hill's cover identity, citing his London criminal associate, the undercover officer. Any link removed from the chain of authentication that established Hill's identity would tend to spook Cahill. Scotland Yard then hit upon the idea of bringing in an American mafioso to convince Cahill and Coyle that Charley Berman had both the money and the organized-crime support to back him up. The "mafioso" was a Baltimore FBI agent who went by the name of Tom Bishop.

Police from different countries often help each other, particularly when they share an interest in the crime or criminals. Irish gangs in New England have close contacts with their counterparts in Ireland, a web made more tangled at the time by IRA gunrunning and fund-raising in the United States. The FBI had active operations against Irish criminals and agreed to help in the sting against Cahill.

Hill told Coyle about Bishop; Coyle told Cahill; Cahill said go ahead. Bishop flew to Dublin. Coyle met him at the airport and took him into the city to a meeting with two Cahill lieutenants. Bishop had a reputation in the FBI as a born performer, which is why they had picked him. Soon he and Cahill's men were all drinking and swapping stories, and Bishop decided to bring out the "proof" of his identity: snapshots dummied up by the FBI that pictured Bishop with John Gotti and other known gangsters. The Irishmen were eagerly pawing through the snaps of famous crooks when a piece of white paper popped out of the pile of photographs. Every eye at the table fell on it. Conversation halted, and the laughter died in their throats. One by one the smiles left the lips of the Irishmen. The paper was a note, of a type that policemen call a confidence slip. This one had the FBI logo printed at the top, and in clear handwriting beneath was the penned reminder: "Tom, don't forget these." As Bishop later told Hill, "They gave me a long look and excused themselves." With Bishop's cover blown, Hill's was too, and the Charley Berman identity was retired for good.

A T ABOUT THIS TIME, Colonel O'Shea's name appeared again in connection with Russborough. It seems that Lady Beit, in the aftermath of the robbery, anxious to have new things on show at the house in the absence of so much of its art, had decided to restore the statuary that Captain Daly had removed from the colonnade in response to the attack by the local priest. When she went looking for the marbles, she could not find them. She ordered a general search of the sheds and outbuildings. The statues did not turn up. In fact, they were no longer at Russborough. O'Shea had packed them off to auction in London. They fetched eighty-two thousand pounds, which O'Shea had split with the gardener, Patrick Teevans. (Teevans's father, Bernard, had worked at the estate before him and helped wreck the statues.) Although O'Shea had shared the proceeds with the younger Teevans, he had not shared it with the Beits.

In October 1987, gardaí arrested Teevans. When he told them

Martin Cahill, aka "The General," in a rare, full-face photograph. (The Sunday World)

how he and O'Shea had recovered the statuary and disposed of it, both men were sent to trial. They denied theft. As O'Shea explained it to the Dublin Circuit Criminal Court, he'd had a "gut feeling" that the statues had been his own property by virtue of his discovery of them, on a tip from the gardener. Lady Beit claimed to have been furious when she confronted the colonel. "For a moment or two he was quite speechless," she told the court. "He said something like, 'The statues were here,' and then blurted out, 'They were in the way so I organized that they should be thrown into Lake Poulaphuca.' To which I replied, 'Well then, get them back from Lake Poulaphuca.' I was very angry." Both men were acquitted, and the colonel went to live in County Kerry.

*   *   *

I N DUBLIN, police no longer had any doubt that Cahill had
robbed the Beits; with the passage of time, the snouts were losing their fear and passing on to detectives what they heard. The
Garda's certainty about Cahill contributed to a sense of humiliation in the force, because the gangster was riding high in criminal
folklore. In the small, relatively homogeneous world of Dublin,
and indeed of Ireland, this celebrity inevitably seeped out into the
general consciousness. Cahill was becoming an outlaw hero. In Ireland you will hear the assertion that a millennium of oppression
has shaped an unloving attitude to authority. This predisposition
fed upon the image of the clever slum lad who had robbed the foreign billionaire and, while he was at it, thumbed his nose at the
Garda. And so it was with particular relish that sixteen months
after the robbery the Garda deputy commissioner, John Paul
McMahon, the second-highest-ranking policeman in the republic,
threw himself into a sting.

The opportunity arose because Cahill, like the Garda, felt frus-
trated and had decided, after the close call with Tom Bishop, to try
again. This second attempt to move the art—an approach to a
crooked Dublin art dealer—opened another chance for the police.

The dealer told Cahill he could not handle paintings as hot as
the Beit collection but knew someone who could. That person was
also an art dealer, with criminal connections, based in London's
"City," the square mile around the Tower that is London's historic
financial center. The City of London retains its ancient borders in
the midst of the metropolitan area, and its own police. Peter
Gwynne, a Scotland Yard detective who had moved to the smaller
City of London force, heard about the feeler from Dublin. Gwynne
turned the London dealer and, with his connivance and the help
of Dutch police, guided Cahill's search to a charming Hollander

named Kees Van Scoaik, a fraud artist, racketeer, and armed robber. Van Scoaik lived in the Dutch city of Arnheim, on the lower Rhine. The information was fed back to Cahill through the turned Londoner that Van Scoaik had deep criminal connections on the Continent and the ability to move high-end items. To demonstrate his good faith, Van Scoaik allegedly paid Cahill's lieutenants ten thousand pounds for Francesco Guardi's *View of the Grand Canal*. If he did, the money came from the Irish police, for the Dutch had turned Van Scoaik and were now, with the Garda and the City of London police, effectively running an agent into the General's midst. The Garda had made this operation possible by paying the Dutch criminal fifty thousand pounds to betray Cahill. The elaborate chain of cooperation among police demonstrated a growing conviction then taking root: that art crime was inherently international, and to fight it required international cooperation.

To prepare for a sting, Deputy Commissioner McMahon set up a dedicated unit of detectives. Mostly they came from the Garda's Special Branch—in effect, spies. They would operate as part of a command established solely for the sting. With strict reporting cutoffs, and isolated from the rest of Garda operations, the unit came under the operational control of the Technical Bureau, a secretive department at Garda headquarters in Phoenix Park.

The sting was set for September 29, 1987, a Tuesday. On the Thursday before, Van Scoaik flew into Dublin. A Garda surveillance team—Van Scoaik's "minders"—was already in place at the airport. They shadowed him into town, making sure that he checked into room 722 in the Burlington Hotel in the Ballsbridge quarter, as arranged. The Technical Bureau had wired the room for sound and installed a video camera in a light.

Van Scoaik soon received a call, inviting him to meet Cahill. The plan called for Van Scoaik to produce one hundred thousand pounds of "show money," the term for a good-faith display of cash meant to establish that a criminal purchaser can supply when required the full amount, in this case one million pounds. In return for the full amount, Van Scoaik was to receive four paintings: the Vermeer, the Gainsborough, the Goya, and a Rubens. Then suddenly the operation hit a snag.

McMahon and his boss, Larry Wren, the Garda commissioner, had gone to a late-night meeting at the Justice Department, the ministry that had to approve the Garda's request for one hundred thousand pounds in Treasury cash. To the policemen's astonishment, the government official refused. He told them that the cabinet would not risk the embarrassment and the political mayhem that would follow if Cahill just grabbed the money and escaped. Profoundly ashamed, the country's senior policemen had to face their Dutch and English colleagues and tell them they could not raise one hundred thousand pounds to rescue a collection valued at the time at one hundred million dollars. The Dutch were incredulous. The operation would have collapsed right then, had not one of the Irish team, on his own initiative, telephoned a bank executive he knew, who agreed to provide a false deposit slip for the sum.

It was Friday. The original timeline for the sting had called for Van Scoaik to show the one hundred thousand pounds to Cahill on Monday, with the swap of the pictures and the full purchase price of one million pounds to take place the day after that, Tuesday, at some place that Cahill had yet to designate. The refusal of the Irish government to supply the cash had now wrecked that plan. For the false deposit slip to take the place of the cash, the show-money stage of the operation had to advance to the weekend, when the banks were closed. Otherwise Cahill would never accept a deposit slip as proof of cash in the bank but would demand the cash itself. It was doubtful he would accept the deposit slip in any case, but the police had no choice except to gamble that he would. At this point, with the operation tottering, the Garda caught a lucky break. Cahill canceled a preliminary meeting scheduled with Van Scoaik for that day.

The news was delivered by Shavo Hogan, a longtime Cahill gangster, who arrived at the hotel to complete negotiations with Van Scoaik. The Dutchman had convinced Cahill that no deal could proceed without Van Scoaik's own art expert examining the pictures—an important detail, because the "expert" was a French detective supplied by Interpol for the sting. The Frenchman would actually get sight of the art and spring the trap. Van Scoaik described the French detective to Hogan and provided details of an allegedly crooked past as an auction-house launderer of stolen art. Hogan accepted this, then told Van Scoaik that Cahill could not make the introductory meeting scheduled for that afternoon. Van Scoaik seized on this as a pretext for demanding a meeting with Cahill the next day, Saturday, rather than waiting until Monday, as Cahill had wanted. Hogan looked doubtful but said he would put it to his boss. He left, and Van Scoaik and his minders waited to see if the General, famously suspicious, would agree.

Cahill did not call that afternoon, nor again that night. Van Scoaik, becoming edgy, wanted to go downstairs to the bar. The hotel operator could forward his calls there, he said. The minders refused. Van Scoaik, who had already spent two thousand pounds in walking-around money, could not walk into a pub without showering drinks on the whole establishment. The Garda had not minded this because they thought the word would get around Dublin and confirm Van Scoaik as a man with cash. But with the operation at a critical point the minders wanted Van Scoaik under tight surveillance, where they could listen in on any phone calls he received. That meant staying in the room.

The waiting dragged on until the middle of the next morning, Saturday, when a Cahill lieutenant called and agreed to move the show-money meeting forward. Cahill would meet Van Scoaik at four o'clock that afternoon, at the Four Roads pub in Crumlin.

Now another problem cropped up. Van Scoaik had run through all his cash. To appear solvent to Cahill, he would need at least one thousand pounds. The Garda could not come up with the money on a Saturday, and one of the Irish minders had to rush out and borrow one thousand pounds on his own from a pub owner he knew.

While this was happening, surveillance officers from the Technical Bureau hurried to the Four Roads pub. They were in place thirty minutes after Cahill's call to the hotel. They took up positions inside and outside the pub, and watched as Cahill's antisurveillance teams arrived and deployed themselves. The environs swarmed with Cahill's people: a man walking his dog in a park across the street, women pushing baby carriages, a pair of laborers fiddling with a manhole cover. The Garda had them all marked.

At the appointed hour, Van Scoaik arrived at the Four Roads pub. Reports of the meeting say Cahill was in a cheerful mood. He did not like the production of a deposit slip instead of cash but accepted Van Scoaik's explanation that he had put the money in the bank for safekeeping when Cahill canceled the Friday meeting. Van Scoaik good-naturedly loaded the tables with drinks. He was perhaps relying on his personal magnetism more than was wise with a man like Cahill, for having departed once from the script, he did so again. Van Scoaik's arrangement with the Irish criminals called for a verification of the paintings' authenticity by an art expert of Van Scoaik's choice. This man, the Dutch criminal now declared, had to return to Paris on Monday and must therefore view and authenticate the pictures on Sunday, the next day.

The mood changed in an instant. Cahill had just swallowed one change—Van Scoaik's deposit slip. To be asked to also shift the schedule ahead shattered the protocol and angered Cahill. He abruptly ended the meeting, telling Van Scoaik he would be in touch, and stalked out with his men. The Garda minders watched the General leave. Within ten minutes Cahill's countersurveillance faded from the Crumlin street. Van Scoaik came out and got in a taxi and drove away.

The Dutchman's mood crumbled. He returned to the hotel in a downcast state. The police already knew what Cahill's reaction had been, because they had been sitting in the Four Roads pub watching the game unfold. The feeling among police when Cahill left the meeting was one of bitter resignation. The government's refusal to supply one hundred thousand pounds in show money had cast inevitable consequences downstream into the operation, and now they were reaping them. The sting was falling apart.

When the phone rang in Van Scoaik's room, it brought a sudden silence. It was the main room number, always kept open for communications from Cahill. The men in the room had not expected a call so soon, if at all. The Garda eavesdroppers put their headsets on and signaled Van Scoaik to answer. Cahill himself was on the line. He set another meeting for that same evening, in the Portobello Road, and told Van Scoaik to be there in an hour. At a signal from the gardaí, Van Scoaik agreed.

As the phone was put back down, the gardaí running the operation knew Cahill had outmaneuvered them. They would never succeed in getting surveillance onto the scene in time; Cahill would have already put his own men into place. Yet they had no choice but to accept the meeting. Cahill seemed to want to complete the deal, and that was a plus for the sting. In fact, Cahill was extremely uneasy and had wanted to abandon the whole scheme. But his chief lieutenants, those who were entitled to share in the proceeds of a sale, and who had yet to receive a penny, had convinced him that Van Scoaik was genuine. The Dutchman's criminal past had been vetted. They reasoned, too, that no police operation would entail such changes of plan. Moreover, they liked him; he was a scoundrel. So Cahill had agreed to proceed with the meeting.

The Portobello Road perfectly suited Cahill's needs. A strip of old towpath separated the street from the Grand Canal. There were trees, and streetlights shed pools of weak, yellowish illumination. A regiment could have concealed itself among the shadows. There was a clear view in every direction. Cahill waited there for Van Scoaik to walk across the bridge, as instructed, turn left, and come along the path until he met them. They had a good look at him as he came, and could find no tail. Cahill stepped into the path and let Van Scoaik come up to him. They completed their arrangements in less than two minutes: Cahill's people would fetch Van Scoaik's expert from the Burlington Hotel at one o'clock in the afternoon the next day, Sunday. If he verified the paintings, Van Scoaik would pay Cahill the full, agreed-upon price of one million pounds.

At the Technical Bureau in Phoenix Park, the mood rose. The news was passed to the deputy commissioner: The sting was on. By dint of luck and the quick thinking of Van Scoaik's minders in the matter of the false-deposit slip, they had a chance to reel in the General. There was tension too. As the top officers knew, the government's near ruin of the operation by withholding the one hundred thousand pounds would not prevent the blame from landing on the Garda if the sting failed.

At noon on Sunday the last instructions were handed down. A "snatch squad" of thirty gardaí—the arrest team—climbed into their vehicles and waited for the order to move. At Dublin airport, the pilot of a police aircraft got his orders and took off. He set his radio to the frequency the Garda had set aside for the sting. The operation would keep to this special frequency, to prevent criminals from detecting the operation by scanning the police bands. If they did, they would hear only routine Garda traffic, made perhaps more reassuring by the extra messages prepared and broadcast by the sting controllers to convince any listeners that the police were thoroughly occupied.

On the dot at one o'clock Shavo Hogan pulled up to the Burlington Hotel in a red Ford Escort. Hogan was wearing a false beard. The French "art expert" came out and got in the car, and Hogan took him on an hour's tour of southside Dublin, cutting through back lanes, making U-turns, threading the streets as he checked for a tail. The Garda stayed on him like glue, one car handing over to another as Hogan dodged and darted through the city. Finally, satisfied he was not being followed, he drove out to Dun Laoghaire, across to Shankill, and went up into the Dublin Mountains.

At Garda headquarters, confidence grew among commanders. They believed they had set an inescapable trap. Even the location was right. They had always thought that was where they would catch their prey. The mountains were Cahill's natural ground. So certain were the gardaí that Cahill would choose these mountains that they had already selected a staging post in the vicinity. As soon as word came back to Phoenix Park that Hogan had finished his evasive measures and was headed for the mountains, the snatch squad went straight to Brigid Burke's pub at Firhouse, a crossroads at the foot of the mountains. An hour and a half had now elapsed since Hogan had driven away from the hotel with the French detective.

At this point, the career of Martin Cahill seemed about to end. The Garda had the General in view. A large force of police— the snatch squad—had gotten to within striking distance of the scene and could move in an instant. Cahill's surveillance had not spotted them. The Garda plane was in position to relay instructions to this force. An intricate series of meetings and contacts from the City of London to Arnheim to the Interpol headquarters in Lyon, France, had all worked in sequence to bring this moment on. Then the whole thing fell apart, in a series of baffling, clownish misadventures.

First the radio started to go wrong. The snatch squad could not hear what the surveillance team was saying; the plane could not hear them either. Nor could the watchers hear the plane. The local gardaí knew that the mountains were riddled with radio "black spots"—places where transmission blanked out. It was one of the features that made the mountains attractive to criminals. But the tactical command had failed to supply a plan to overcome this crucial deficit. As the police communications were failing, Hogan and the Frenchman were arriving at Kilakee Wood, only three miles from the Garda force massed below at Firhouse.

At the edge of the wood, Cahill and Eamon Daly, a Cahill protégé, met Hogan's car. They led the French detective into the trees, an action witnessed by Garda surveillance. That section of the range is forested, which had given cover to the Garda tail. But the trees gave cover to Cahill too.

In the wood, Cahill produced the four pictures. The French detective had a radio concealed in a flashlight. Upon seeing the paintings, he hauled out his device and swept the beam back and forth across the pictures and loudly announced, "They are the real thing. They are the real thing." The police plane could not hear him. "They are the real thing," he boomed again.

Cahill smelled a trap. He and Daly grabbed the paintings and bundled them back to the road. Hogan took the Frenchman by the arm, shoved him into the car, and tore away from the scene. The Garda tail got back on him after he went racing past their position. Cahill and Daly stowed the paintings in their car and fled the scene.

The route that Cahill took led down into Firhouse, and as he came to Brigid Burke's he saw the Garda vehicles pulled over at the side and the force of armed police. At that moment, the snatch squad's commander was inside the pub, using the phone to call

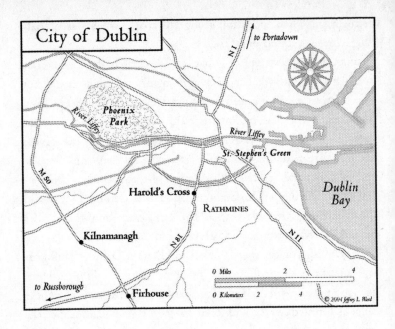

City of Dublin

to Portadown

Phoenix Park

River Liffey

River Liffey

St. Stephen's Green

Harold's Cross

RATHMINES

Dublin Bay

Kilnamanagh

to Russborough

Firhouse

0 Miles 2 4

0 Kilometers 2 4

© 2004 Jeffrey L. Ward

operational control at Phoenix Park. He was told that Cahill and the gang were in a wood in the mountains just above them.

Cahill and Daly were driving slowly past the pub. "Take it nice and easy," Cahill is reported to have said, and then when they had passed, "We're all right; they must be looking for the IRA."

Moments later the order came through for the snatch squad to seize the wood. They surged up the road and poured out of their vehicles into the trees at the point the General had just abandoned. The trap sprang shut on nothing. Gardaí pulled over Hogan as he came into Shankill, and arrested him under the Offenses Against the State Act. Two days later they had to let him go.

The Vermeer went into an attic in the suburb of Tallaght.

Recriminations rose up in the dust of the collapsed sting. In the Irish government, some privately derided the operation; the failure to retrieve the Beit gift plainly incensed them. By contrast, Cahill's reputation soared. He had escaped capture not by his wits but by the blunders of police. Yet the word in the pubs was that he was invincible and had outfoxed the gardaí at every turn. He had made them a laughingstock.

{ 6 }

The Tango Squad

THE YEAR THAT CAHILL LEFT the Garda milling haplessly through the woods above Firhouse was a great year for Irish crime. A plague of armed robberies swept the country: some six hundred separate crimes, five hundred in Dublin alone. The Garda solved one hundred of them. Cahill blazed his own fiery trail through this firmament, busting into houses and binding the occupants and carting off their valuables while they sat roped in their chairs, terrified. A torrent of abuse poured into the Phoenix Park Garda headquarters from the capital's wealthy victims.

A lover of the night, Cahill would often slip out alone in the dark hours, telling no one of his errand. He thrilled to the work of the "creeper," the lone break-and-enter man who burglarizes a home while its inhabitants sleep. It added to his pleasure that the Garda had him targeted. He relished diving into the Dublin streets with the police tailing him, finally to lose them, and while they were sniffing up and down the empty streets for his scent, to open a window and go in.

The General loved working alone. In the criminal world, betrayal is a staple currency. Although Cahill's gang had a reputation for impenetrability, he was suspicious of them all. He believed in vengeance, a fact well known; fear was a more reliable bond of silence than loyalty. When a Dubliner named Anthony Quinn was acquitted on grounds of self-defense of the murder of Cahill's obscenely violent younger brother, Paddy, he hurried from the courthouse, packed, and sailed for England. That night Cahill razed his house.

One chronicler says Cahill's organizational talents and the appetite of his underlings for loot led him to chair weekly meetings at which the gang planned robberies, as many as three a week. But that is absurd. Cahill was much too careful. Regular assemblies of Dublin blackguards, as if they were the board of General Motors, does not fit with Cahill's well-documented fearfulness. Matching his tactical skills was a lively paranoia. He believed, for example, that because Sir Alfred Beit had connections to South Africa, that country's Bureau of State Security, a spy agency with a reputation for a long reach, had decreed his assassination.

Cahill mastered these fears. In the aftermath of the Garda's failed sting he liked to cruise by the police security post outside the home of Garret FitzGerald, the prime minister, and stop and smile at the gardaí there. Once at a checkpoint he told a policeman, "Youse made a mistake. Youse brought the wrong gardaí," a reference to the bitter feuding inside the Garda, where some were saying openly that the operation against the General should have been run, not by the Special Branch and the Technical Bureau, but by the criminal units—the true, the natural adversaries of Cahill. It was during this fractious period that a new Garda commissioner came into the top job.

E AMON DOHERTY could scarcely have come from a background more different from Cahill's. His father had been a wealthy cattle dealer in County Donegal, with enough money to send

Eamon Doherty
(Irish Times)

his son to St. Columba's, an exclusive private school in Derry. In 1944, as a young man with an eye on a career, Doherty applied to both the Garda and the Customs and Excise section of the Revenue Commissioners. Both applications were successful, but he picked the Garda because it had answered first.

Doherty rose steadily if unspectacularly through the ranks. He was the first Garda officer to train with the FBI—a management course. He built a reputation as an administrator, became a chief superintendent at Dublin Castle, rose to assistant commissioner, and, one year later, in 1979, thirty-four years after enlisting, was appointed deputy commissioner, the second-highest Garda rank. His responsibilities were administration and finance, but his political masters seemed to want his steady, manager's hand close to the wheel, because the Garda was in crisis.

That year both IRA prisoners and ordinary criminals had begun to bring charges of brutality against the Garda. The so-called Heavy Gang drew most of the charges. What is more, some gardaí, unhappy with what they saw as harassment of political targets, confirmed the charges. At the same time, the Association of Garda Sergeants and Inspectors (AGSI) had started to clamor against political interference in police affairs. So suspicious of the high command was AGSI that it had started sweeping its offices for bugs. Smoothing this turbulence was an important task for the men who then succeeded to the Garda's top positions—Larry Wren, commissioner, and his deputy, Doherty. Together, they ushered in a period of stability that lasted seven years. It ended with a sharp increase in criminal activity. In 1987 Wren retired, and Doherty became commissioner.

Ireland's senior policeman works from an enormous suite with a splendid view of the parade ground and the main gates, and the trees and meadows of Phoenix Park beyond. Not far away is the old Vice-Regal Lodge, once a symbol of Britain's colonial rule and now the residence of the president of Ireland. The American ambassador's house is a stroll away across the green. In the normal course of his official life, Doherty's long, black car would drop him off at either of these centers of Irish power. He had arrived. Unhappily for Doherty, he had little time to luxuriate in the perquisites of his position.

The insignia of Doherty's new rank had barely begun to twinkle on his shoulders when, on October 28, 1987, French customs agents boarded a small coasting vessel, the *Eksund*, off the Brittany coast. In its hold they found one thousand Romanian-made AK-47 assault rifles, some million rounds of ammunition, 430 grenades, twelve RPGs (launchers for rocket-propelled grenades), more than fifty SAM-7 shoulder-fired ground-to-air missiles, assorted flamethrowers and antitank guns, and two tons of Semtex, a Czech-made plastic

The Tango Squad

explosive. The entire terrifying cargo had originated in Libya and was headed for Ireland. It belonged to the IRA. Worse, Irish intelligence discovered, and the press reported, that four other similar cargoes had already been landed.

The news that an IRA gunrunning pipeline had been gushing weapons into the republic ignited a crisis. In a sense, Ireland was a country at war with itself. The leadership in Dublin favored, at least nominally, the union of the whole of Ireland. The IRA wanted the same thing but was ready to fight for it. Support for the IRA was not deep in Ireland. Most citizens preferred political solutions to essentially political problems. Even in the six counties of Northern Ireland, the IRA had relatively few committed members. But the old, republican cause still resonated powerfully in the emotions of some of the Irish, and the revelation that the IRA was awash in fire-power shocked the police. The guerrillas' main source of weapons, the United States, had dried up in 1985, when the FBI in New York City infiltrated and broke up the mafia-connected gunrunning ring operated by George Harrison, a veteran IRA soldier from County Mayo. Only two years later, the IRA had found another source: Libya. The *Eksund* affair demanded a swift response, and in a single day the Garda, bolstered by army troops, raided sixty thousand locations. The raids were a bust: The weapons had disappeared into secret arsenals.

WHILE THE GARDA reeled from the aftermath of the *Eksund*, ordinary crime continued to increase rapidly. To deal with the mounting threat, Doherty convened a meeting of every chief superintendent in the Dublin metropolitan area. On December 2, 1987, he walked from his huge, red-carpeted office into the adjoining boardroom; the instructions he gave his senior officers were marvelously terse. He wanted a list of every criminal target in the capital. All police intelligence on the targets must be cobbled into this new list. When the dossier was complete, they would meet again, assess the strength and vulnerability of each target, and assign priority. There was not much doubt whose name would top the list, but as if to make sure that they put it there, Cahill chose this moment to strike again.

On the evening of November 30, less than a month after Doherty's summons to commanders, Cahill's men smashed their way into a house in Inchicore, a west Dublin suburb. The postmistress at Kilnamanagh, Anne Gallagher, lived in the house. The gangsters seized Gallagher and her landlady, Nellie Whelan, manhandled them into a car, and sped away. The kidnappers took the women to an address in Tallaght. Other gangsters had already stormed the Tallaght house, and the owner, Myles Crofton, was hostage inside with his family.

That night Cahill's men strapped a bomb to Crofton's chest, explaining to the postmistress how it worked, and what it would do to Crofton and anybody near him if it went off. They wired a radio detonator into the explosives and showed the hostages how that worked too. In the morning they gave Gallagher her instructions. With Crofton in tow, she would open the Kilnamanagh post office, take thirty thousand pounds in stamps and cash out of the till, and bring it all back to Tallaght. The gang made Crofton take along his eighteen-month-old daughter. Gallagher followed the instructions and gave the money and the stamps to the thieves, who released the hostages and drove away.

The crime struck the Garda like a slap in the face. It was a public humiliation, delivered in the spotlight of the press. Innocent citizens, including an infant, had been pulled from their homes and put in peril of their lives. The crime stoked anger in the police rank and file, who soon learned Cahill had done it. The day of the robbery, December 1, 1987, Ned Ryan, by then a detec-

Phoenix Park Garda headquarters (Matthew Hart)

tive superintendent, the man who had predicted Cahill would end up stealing old ladies' handbags, was furious at Cahill's apparent impunity. The only way to destroy him, insisted Ryan, was to set up a squad tasked with breaking Cahill, and nothing else. His boss agreed and called the commissioner.

The following day at ten o'clock in the morning Commissioner Doherty walked through into the third-floor boardroom to meet, for the second time in thirty days, his entire top command. The files on the republic's most notorious criminals sat on the big table, but Doherty did not ask about them. He pulled out his chair and sat down and looked around the table and said, "What are we going to do about this man Cahill?"

O UT OF THE MEETING that December morning came one of the most famous police units in Irish history: the Tango squad. In the parlance of English-language radio operators, *Tango* means the letter *T*. In this case the *T* stood for *Target*. The meeting at Phoenix Park had made Cahill the primary target of the Garda, which assigned him the code name Tango One. The mission of the squad was to destroy Cahill.

The main criminal detective unit of the Garda is quartered at Harcourt Square, a Stalinesque monstrosity on Harcourt Street in central Dublin. Three large, redbrick buildings loom behind an iron fence. Overall command at Harcourt Square was in the hands of Detective Chief Superintendent John Murphy. Murphy's operational responsibilities were too broad for him to focus only on a single operation, and he shared the daily running of the Tango squad with his deputy, a policeman with a high place in Garda lore—Detective Superintendent Noel Conroy.

Conroy is a man of medium height, with intense, dark-blue eyes and a wolfish grin. Gardaí who know him say he routinely works fourteen-hour days and has the focus of a chess master. On Monday, December 7, five days after the second meeting in Doherty's office, some ninety gardaí packed themselves into a conference room with Conroy and his boss. Many of them were new recruits, selected because they had as yet no other operational duties to deflect them from the task that Murphy and Conroy described—a crushing surveillance to be piled upon Cahill.

In the five preceding days, Conroy had helped to form the principal tactical decision of the planned surveillance: It would be entirely visible to Cahill. There would be no subterfuge. The gardaí would sit on him in plain sight until he could not breathe. They would sit on Shavo Hogan and Eamon Daly and other Cahill associates until the criminals concluded that the price of membership in the General's gang was the strangulation of their livelihood. The young gardaí were told that Cahill and the others would try to find

Noel Conroy
(Irish Times)

out who they were and where they lived, and would not hesitate to threaten their families.

For three weeks the gardaí of the Tango squad took special training. They reported daily to the practice range; they mastered an arsenal of weapons. (Constables in Ireland do not routinely carry arms.) They drilled day after day in the art of high-speed pursuit, tearing over the Garda's driving courses and threading pylons at top speed. They suffered impacts from other cars and learned to deliver them.

While the recruits trained, Conroy and Murphy sent an unusual embassy to the criminal. A plainclothes officer from the central detective unit, a man known to Cahill, drove up beside him on the street, got out of his car, and stopped Cahill. The policeman smiled pleasantly and asked him how he was. As usual, Cahill made no reply. The detective then told him that the Beit paintings must be returned within three days. He said Cahill could pick the location, as long as he let the Garda know where to pick them up. That's what they wanted, he told the General: the pictures. If Cahill did not produce them in the stipulated time, the Garda would take further action. Then he got back in his car and drove away.

This encounter is said to have rattled Cahill, which can have been its only aim. No one expected him to return the pictures. This was the first shot in the new war.

On Christmas Eve the Tango squad, weeded down to seventy, went into the streets of Dublin. They grabbed Eamon Daly as he came out of the Rathmines Inn and made him take a Breathalyzer test. He passed, but when he went to get his car he found the tires slashed. The slashing of tires was a trademark Cahill act, often against the cars of gardaí. Cahill was now to learn that a different day had dawned. For on Christmas Day he saw, parked in plain view across the street from his house in Cowper Downs, a car with a pair of large young men in Garda uniform sitting in it, beaming back at him. They even waved.

THE TANGO SQUAD began to follow Cahill everywhere, sometimes trailing along behind him in a cavalcade of cars. If he dropped into a pub, he would find the table next to him filling with police, who took no trouble to conceal their identities, but instead watched him and smiled at him, or wiggled their fingers in greeting. There is an account of Cahill's car being stopped by a detective, who leaned down and said to Cahill, "Martin, me old flower, it's only a matter of time now before we have you. But fair play to you, you had a good run of it." To which Cahill roared back, "Youse are all criminals! Youse are worse than the fuckin' robbers themselves!"

Cahill struck back. In less than a month members of his gang had approached five different members of the Tango squad and recited the names of their wives and, if they had them, children. Cahill himself sometimes drove up to the homes of gardaí detailed to watch him, and crept slowly past with his hazard lights flashing. It made no difference to Cahill that even as he did so there were gardaí following him; he relished the chance to display his defiance. At his home he would sometimes come out of the house and cross the street to the parked gardaí and videotape them as they sat there looking back. Some of the Tango officers took to keeping guns beside them as they slept. They carefully examined their cars for booby traps before opening the doors. The Garda moved some officers' families to secret locations. At least a dozen of the Tango men grew beards and took to wearing dark glasses to conceal their identities from Cahill's men.

Cahill ambushed his antagonists. He had a talented young driver—a wheelman—who was keen to prove himself. They laid a simple plan. Cahill waited until there was a single surveillance car parked in front of his house. Then he emerged in a hurry and went off in his Mercedes, drawing the gardaí along behind. He went this way and that through the city, cutting back on his tail, then cutting back again, so that any backup surveillance summoned by radio would be ceaselessly thrown off course by new, conflicting instructions. Finally, he led the Tango car into a public-housing complex, where the wheelman waited. As Cahill lured the gardaí past a dark lane, the young driver rocketed out in a stolen car and rammed the police vehicle, disabling it. Freed of surveillance, Cahill sped off.

He had other tricks too. Once, returning from a morning errand, Cahill's wife, Frances, with Cahill in the passenger seat, backed the car into the garage. Cahill remained in the car for seven hours. When the car next came out, with only Frances visible, the gardaí assumed that Tango One was still inside the house. Frances drove away with Cahill lying flat on the back floor.

Sometimes the contest degenerated into farce. The gardaí took any vantage point to spy on the General, even climbing into trees. One night in February a Tango garda, ensconced in high branches in a neighbor's yard, spied a black shape squirming along the ground. He shone his flashlight down and saw it was Cahill. When the beam of the flashlight caught him, Cahill lay motionless. He stayed there for six hours, until dawn. Then he got up and walked into his house.

He tried to evade surveillance using his motorcycle too. Cahill was an expert rider. He would start up his bike inside his garage, then nod to one of his children, who would heave up the door. Cahill would explode from the garage and surprise the Tango gardaí, who sometimes failed to get after him in time and lost him. "Yes," said Noel Conroy when I asked him about the motorcycle, "he did that for a bit. He had that big Harley." Conroy had a sheaf of notes in his hand at the time, which he'd been consulting as we spoke. But this time he didn't look at them. He smiled his dark smile as he recalled the game. "We put a stop to that, though, didn't we. I put a young lad on an 1100-cc Honda, and next thing you know your man Cahill lost it on a corner and smashed his leg, and that was the end of that."

And so it went. Cahill's men dug holes in the Garda golf course at Stackstown and slashed the tires on a score of Garda cars. Cahill's own car was trashed in turn, and his henchman, Eamon Daly, came out one day to find his tires, for a second time, literally hacked to bits. Shavo Hogan punched a garda in the face. Cahill, his wife, Frances, and her sister, Tina Lawless, were arrested on a weapons charge. Cahill was later released, then immediately rearrested as he left the Bridewell Garda station. He was charged with failing to keep

The Tango Squad

the peace. Instead of locking him up in Dublin, they sent him to Spike Island, a prison in Cork Harbor, and kept him there three months. They caught his older brother, John, in the midst of a robbery. The Dublin Criminal Court, in a black mood, sent him to Portalaoise prison for sixteen years.

It was starting to be heard in the Dublin demimonde that the Beit pictures were a curse, that nothing good had come of them and much bad. Cahill's lieutenants were disappearing into prison one by one. As his fame as a crime lord grew and he became the subject of articles and documentaries, this added another layer of surveillance, that of the press. To repair his dwindling fortunes, Cahill hit upon an idea that was both bold and desperate: another art theft.

The victim was Alice Murnaghan, the ninety-two-year-old widow of a supreme court judge. She came from an old Dublin financial family and lived in a mansion on Fitzwilliam Street, in a spic-and-span quarter of Georgian houses, street after street of them standing on parade immaculately dressed. The duke of Wellington was born a block from Fitzwilliam Street, when his father, the earl of Mornington, was helping the Irish run their country. Murnaghan's late husband had been something of a grandee himself, and the house contained a fortune in paintings and other precious objects.

It seems amazing that Cahill managed to shake the Tango squad, but he did. He got clear away, and at ten o'clock on the night of December 7, 1988, he and a pair of low-level crooks idled into Lad Lane in a stolen van and drew up alongside Murnaghan's back wall. They scaled the wall, disabled the alarm, broke in through the basement, grabbed the housekeeper, and hustled her upstairs to the vast, becurtained bedroom, where the elderly lady of the house sat reading. The story has it that Cahill treated Murnaghan gallantly, fetching her tea and biscuits while his colleagues went through the place and stole some sixty paintings and a sackful of silver.

The caper ended badly for Cahill. He had had an English fence lined up, but the man, who had intended to ransom the paintings to the insurance company, backed out when he found there wasn't one. Six weeks after the robbery the Garda pounced on two of Cahill's men when they tried to retrieve part of the loot, buried beside a convent in Mount Merrion. Forty of the paintings were recovered within two weeks.

The landscape was getting bleak for the General. Since the Tango squad had fastened onto him, ten of his seasoned henchmen had gone off to prison. His best asset, the Beit pictures, lay secreted uselessly in Dublin and the Wicklow Mountains—priceless booty that had brought Cahill not money but a ruinous harassment. At bay, he launched another bid to sell the paintings.

IN DUBLIN LIVED a man named John Naughton, not at first a criminal but a victim of crime. Cahill had robbed his house. When he later learned that Naughton was a "decent bloke," and newly unemployed, the gangster had, if you care to believe it, returned Naughton's things. However it transpired, Cahill enlisted Naughton in an attempt to sell the Beit hoard. After an initial call to a London art dealer was rebuffed (Naughton had offered him the Gainsborough), he decided to try again.

Naughton was unskilled in the criminal arts. Having perhaps an idée fixe about this dealer, he flew to London in the spring of 1989 and called him again. Naughton could not know it, but his arrival in London coincided with the reestablishment by Scotland Yard of the Art and Antiques squad.

The policeman detailed to set up the new unit and run it was a short, sturdy detective sergeant named Dick Ellis. These days Ellis

The Tango Squad

Dick Ellis (From the collection of Dick Ellis)

runs *Trace*, a magazine and database that supplies art-market and art-crime intelligence. He lives in an old market town in Hertford-shire, from which he ranges the countryside after stolen pictures and antiques. In London he works from a tiny office—a four-flight climb up narrow stairs to the attic. Sitting there in the clutter, Ellis does not look the part of a famous detective, but in his world he is. He has masterminded some of the neatest stings in art crime, including the operation that recovered Pieter Brueghel the Elder's *Christ and the Woman Taken in Adultery*, stolen from London's Courtauld Institute.

Ellis came into the Russborough story after Naughton made his second call to the London dealer. "He made an odd proposal to the man he'd spoken to before," Ellis explained. "He told him he had a client who wanted him to authenticate eleven paintings, that they were the Beit pictures, and that he, the London dealer, should fly to Dublin, where he'd be taken to several different locations to see the paintings. If he did that, and authenticated them, Naughton's client would pay him five hundred thousand pounds into a Swiss account. If he refused to come and see the works, he'd get a bullet in the head." Ellis spread his hands. "It's not the usual kind of proposal."

Instead of flying to Dublin, the man called Scotland Yard. Ellis told him to go ahead and agree to meet Naughton in a few days. Naughton was staying in a flat in Cleveland Square, in fashionable Notting Hill. When the dealer called Ellis back with the address, Ellis called in Scotland Yard technicians. They gained entry to the floor above, and when Naughton was out, wired his flat for sound. Then Ellis called in SO-19, the specialist firearms unit—policemen with the kind of weapons suitable for a major firefight.

"We didn't know what we were going to find," said Ellis. "Naughton was Irish, and there'd been lots of speculation about the Beit collection that Irish paramilitaries might get into the movement of the pictures. He'd said they'd put a bullet in the contact's head. We didn't know what backup he might have. If it was the IRA, they would definitely have backup. So we concealed a force around the building."

On the appointed day the dealer arrived at the flat, knocked, and Naughton let him in. Upstairs, Ellis listened to the conversation. Naughton restated the deal, and the dealer agreed to go with him. They stepped outside to the street. Ellis gave the signal, and a dozen officers sprang from their places and overwhelmed Naughton, crushing him to the pavement. Naughton later refused to betray Cahill but did confirm that his "client" had planned to use the authentication to extort a ransom of ten million pounds from the paintings' owners.

To Ellis, this proved the naïveté of the thieves, because the Irish government owned the paintings, and governments do not pay ransom. The Naughton scheme had never had a hope of succeeding, not least because of Naughton's lack of criminal knowledge. Even the name of the art dealer he'd approached had come to him from an innocent source: his brother.

"The brother was a landscape painter," Ellis said, "and of course we went to see him. He lived in Scotland, in a cottage beside the royal estate at Balmoral. From his window he could watch the queen mother salmon-fishing. As it turned out, he'd met the art dealer in a legitimate picture transaction. He'd had no idea what his brother was up to. He was completely shocked. We could see how upset he was. After we talked to him we offered to buy him a drink at the local pub, and he said, 'No thanks. I'm going to go up into the mountains and have a cry.'"

Naughton went to prison for two years. It seems unlikely that Cahill's hopes had ever been pinned to him too firmly, for by the end of 1989, while Naughton still awaited trial, another attempt to move the Beit pictures had already been in train for a year. This time the agent was an accomplished criminal: Tommy Coyle.

COYLE HAD NEVER given up on the Beit collection. He had engineered five different schemes to sell the art. Among his plans had been an approach to the IRA. They were a logical choice for Coyle because of their international connections, particularly in the United States, and because they had expertise in the ways that stolen objects are exchanged for other stolen objects, such as guns. Nothing came of the contact, probably because Cahill and the IRA hated each other.

"There was an antagonism between them," according to Paddy Prendeville, editor of the Dublin satirical magazine *Phoenix*. "They were two underground armies, basically, one political and the other just criminal. One of Cahill's men was a drug pusher in the part of Dublin where I lived, and the IRA decided to take him out. I wrote about it, and the next thing I knew two IRA guys showed up at my house, saying 'Who the fuck told you that?' They didn't want to get into a gun battle with Cahill. It's OK to whack away at the Brits up north, but they didn't want to upset the authorities in the republic [by starting a shooting war in Dublin]."

When the IRA declined the Beit paintings, Coyle contacted the Ulster Volunteer Force (UVF), a Northern Ireland loyalist militia, and therefore Protestant. The UVF was definitely interested, and Cahill gave Coyle permission to open negotiations. It was a reckless act, sure to infuriate the IRA, who were bound to discover it. Moreover, dealings with the UVF were inherently risky: As a paramilitary group they were spied upon ferociously by both the British and the Garda's Special Branch.

Coyle lived near Drogheda, a town twenty-five miles north of Dublin. The UVF contacts came from Portadown—in County Armagh in Northern Ireland—some fifty miles north of Drogheda. The main highway north from Dublin, the N1, runs up through Drogheda and Dundalk to Newry, and from there you can take a major road to either Belfast or Portadown. It's hard to think of any route on Earth that would be more scrutinized, except perhaps the road from Gaza to Tel Aviv, but it was the N1 the UVF men used. Of course the Garda saw them.

"Well I had a special unit watching Cahill," Noel Conroy said, "and we knew he had contact with Coyle. Then we saw these people coming down from Portadown. It's unusual to see criminals in Dublin getting involved with loyalists in Northern Ireland, but in our experience if there's money to be made they're pretty quickly prepared to deal."

Conroy put his people onto the Ulstermen, and soon the police observed the militiamen return back up the N1. From an informant inside Cahill's gang, Garda agents learned that the UVF had bought a painting. The agents did not know which one but thought it was one of the Beits'. "We watched very carefully the movement of certain people," Conroy said. "We got intelligence from certain sources that the painting had moved to Turkey. We'd intelligence that certain Northern Ireland loyalist paramilitary people had been in and out of Turkey. I'd been in touch with a Turkish policeman I'd met in Lyon [at Interpol headquarters], and I alerted him that a certain painting might very well be in a certain hotel."

Conroy's manner of speech, with a "certain" this and a "certain" that, is the natural habit of a policeman guarding his sources. But the opacity of his expression perfectly suited the situation he was describing, for Cahill, by dealing with the UVF, had entered murky territory.

Ireland has been the playground of a dozen outlaw groups and the agents of many countries. The traffic in arms alone has peopled the island with blackguards from everywhere: South Africans buying missile parts stolen from the Shorts factory in Belfast, Libyans running guns, American sympathizers of the IRA, British spies as thick on the ground as broadloom. No doubt this carnival has shut down some of its rides since the entry of the Sinn Féin Party, the political side of the IRA, into the most recent process launched by the British and Irish governments to bring peace to Northern Ireland; although such venomous rumps as the Real IRA continue to wage war in Ireland, the cause of violent republicanism has dwindled. But at the time Cahill was dealing with the UVF, the scene was a darker one. To help me understand what that might have meant for Cahill, Paddy Prendeville of the *Phoenix* suggested I meet one of his writers, a foxy veteran of espionage reporting named Frank Doherty.

Doherty, a man of about sixty, has a charming and infectious way about him, a vast disdain for the British, and a hearty appetite for speculation. "Ask yourself," he said, as we were discussing the UVF and the painting, "how some Northern Irish yob from Portadown has a clue how to sell a Dutch old-master painting to a Turk."

"I guess he had a contact."

"And who would give him that?"

"Someone who supported his cause?"

"Sure, and his *cause*," said Doherty, dragging out the word, "might be generally given as screwing the IRA."

"So you're saying the contact would be someone who wanted to help them against the IRA?"

"I am."

In Doherty's scenario, British intelligence had supplied the UVF with the Turkish contact, since the UVF were British proxies in the contest with the IRA. The British motive would simply have been to help the UVF get money to buy arms. Doherty's cloak-and-dagger plot theory is not the only way to view events. After all, the UVF were criminals, and criminals do not need spies to put them in touch with other criminals. But Doherty's opinion does show what treacherous ground Cahill had stepped onto, and how easily his actions could take on a political coloration.

On a February day in 1990, acting on Conroy's information, Turkish police crashed through a hotel-room door in Istanbul. They found the UVF handing over to Turkish buyers Gabriel Metsu's *A Woman Reading a Letter*, one of two Metsus stolen by Cahill.

The Metsu was the first painting recovered from the 1986 raid, and the news splashed into the Irish press. It had become an open secret that Cahill was the Russborough thief, and the Turkish story immediately lowered his standing with the public. The UVF connection revealed him to be not a Robin Hood but a man prepared to deal for his own gain with Northern Irish Protestant loyalists—men despised by the overwhelmingly Catholic population of the republic. After all, the guns the loyalists would buy by selling pictures stolen from the Irish people would be used to kill Catholics. A man spinning such schemes could only earn contempt.

T HE METSU CAME HOME in style. Sergio Benedetti, a curator at the National Gallery of Ireland, flew to Istanbul to supervise the packing. The painting rode back in its own seat, next to Benedetti. He carried it himself through London airport when he transferred to the Aer Lingus flight to Dublin. Andrew O'Connor drove to the Dublin airport to meet Benedetti at eleven at night. They took the Metsu back to the conservation studio but did not unpack it.

O'Connor gave the picture a full day to acclimatize before he took it from the packing case and unwrapped it. Since it was the first Beit picture to be recovered from the Cahill raid, he did not know what condition he would find it in. He feared the worst, because the painting had traveled from Dublin to Northern Ireland and by unknown routes to Istanbul. "I opened the packing," O'Connor said, "and right away I could see there was paint loss. In the top right-hand corner a triangular piece had completely broken off, and was gone. In the end, though, I was pretty relieved. It could have been a lot worse. When you think of the care we take when we ship a painting, and think what this one had gone through, you could have expected a lot more damage."

The Metsu survived the Turkish adventure in better shape than Cahill. Four years had passed since he had robbed Sir Alfred Beit. His reputation had been muddied by dealing with the UVF. The Tango gardaí had reduced his gang to an ad hoc rabble. The great treasure of the Beit collection sat moldering in holes instead of enriching him. Now another crime, three thousand miles away, in Boston, was to raise the value of the stakes in Cahill's Vermeer and lead the General into a final gambit to get rid of it.

{ 7 }

Mrs. Gardner's House

ALMOST 150 YEARS EARLIER, on April 14, 1840, Isabella
Stewart was born in New York City. She was the first child
of a rising young businessman, David Stewart, and his wife, Adelia
Smith. The Smith side of the family descended from a Long Island
settler named "Bull" Smith, who founded Smithtown. The story
was told that when Smith bought his land from Indians, they said
he could have whatever he could ride around in a day, and he
climbed on his bull and off he went. Isabella always treasured the
idea of her ancestor charging through the woods on a bull, but it
was another Long Islander, her grandmother and namesake, who
played a larger role in shaping her.

Isabella Tod Stewart was a redoubtable Scottish lady, widowed
long before her granddaughter's birth, who managed with a firm
hand her large estate at Jamaica, Long Island. She bred prize cattle
and won ribbons for her flowers and held a pew at the local Episco-
pal church. She also had a titanic temper, which perfectly matched
that of her tiny grandchild, and they battled from the moment
Isabella was old enough to pronounce the word *no*. Mrs. Stewart
could pronounce it, too, and did one day when the rebellious
Isabella, banished temporarily to Long Island by her exhausted

parents, demanded to go to a circus that had pitched its tents nearby. When her grandmother refused, she marched off on her own, and the butler was dispatched to bring her back. When she saw him coming, Isabella tore off as fast as her legs could carry her. The butler was forced to abandon his customary dignity and pound along in hot pursuit. He caught her just as she was scrambling under a circus tent. He seized her by the ankles and dragged her out and slung her over his shoulder as she screamed with fury.

To her regret, Isabella did not resemble her striking grandmother. Because she was so plain, Isabella took pains with what she had. She guarded her fine, pale skin, which would freckle in the slightest touch of sun. At Jamaica she learned to ride a horse. In New York, her father saw to it that she added French to her accomplishments, along with music and dancing. David Stewart was advancing rapidly in business. He got into steel and made himself a millionaire. When his daughter turned sixteen, he took her to France to be "finished." There she met Julia Gardner.

The bluest New England blood ran in the Gardners' veins. To match their pedigree, they had a banking and trading fortune and a mansion in Boston's Beacon Hill. They also had a bachelor son, John Lowell Gardner Jr.—Jack—twenty-one, a yachtsman and, in the family tradition, a financier. Even as a young man, Jack Gardner displayed the level demeanor expected of a New England prince. The debutantes he met showed equally proper reserve. Julia Gardner's friend from New York broke upon this scene with hectic abandon. There was snow in Boston when Isabella arrived, and she and Julia commandeered a horse-drawn sleigh called Cleopatra's Barge and went caroming around on Boston Common. In dinnertable conversation she eagerly took part. She was eighteen when she came to Boston and nineteen when, in 1859, she married Jack.

Isabella Stewart Gardner's life looked as if it would follow a conventional path. Two years after they were married, the young couple built a mansion on Beacon Street. Soon they had a son: John Lowell Gardner III, called Jackie. A month after Jackie's birth, Isabella's sister-in-law, Julia, who had married Randolph Coolidge, had a second son, and a few months after that Jack Gardner's elder brother and his wife, Harriet, had a second baby too, also a boy. All three families lived on Beacon Street, and Isabella saw a future in which the three cousins would grow to manhood in the bosom of their extended family.

This happy world crumbled less than two years later. Jackie took ill, slid into an unstoppable decline, and died of pneumonia. In her grief, Isabella would not allow anyone to touch the boy. She dressed his body herself and combed his hair a final time.

When her next pregnancy ended in miscarriage, Isabella's spirit cracked, and at the age of twenty-five she took to her bed and descended into a pit from which no one could raise her. The Gardners tried everything, sending in a parade of eminent doctors to see her. Nothing worked; Isabella was shut tight against the world. Month led into month, and she would not leave her room. She stayed there two full years, until at last, in desperation, Jack Gardner had her carried from the house on her mattress, and down to a ship, and took her off to Europe.

It was a masterstroke. Sailing from Boston, Isabella left her grief behind. In Paris the Gardners found a city frothing with the diversions of the Second Empire. One of these was fashion, much of it from a single salon in the rue de Paix, where Englishman Charles Worth had banished the hoops that had hidden women's shapes for a century.

The French empress, Eugénie, was among Worth's clients, and he rarely came out of his workroom for lesser women. But he liked what he'd heard about the young Americans, and when Isabella and Jack showed up he wrapped a silk dressing gown around his baggy smock and, with a pair of spaniels padding at his heels, issued from his atelier. It was love at first sight for the aging designer and the young woman with the fresh, bold gaze. When the Gardners returned to Boston eighteen months later, the radiant creature who came surging off the ship on her husband's arm was ablaze in Worth's designs, and New England's merchant aristocracy gained its first glimpse of what would become, from that moment, Isabella's chief creation: herself.

RANSACKING BOSTON for diversions, Isabella met Charles Eliot Norton, the literary populist and lecturer. A Boston Brahmin himself, Norton in the late 1870s urged Isabella to focus her energy on collecting. She did, and for the next forty-five years the stream of art and artists flowing into the Gardners' home captivated her contemporaries. John Singer Sargent painted her in a low-cut, black dress with a rope of pearls at her waist and a voluptuous tapestry behind her. There were whispers of scandal, possibly not groundless. Ellery Sedgwick, who later became editor of the *Atlantic Monthly*, recorded a scene he had witnessed as a schoolboy at Groton, when Isabella had brought Sargent out to show him the school.

"I was buried in my book, when suddenly the gymnasium door was thrown wildly open and a woman's voice thrilled me with a little scream of mockery and triumph. I peeked from my concealment and caught sight of a woman with a figure of a girl, her modish muslin skirt fluttering behind her as she dashed through the doorway and flew across the floor, tossing over her shoulder some taunting paean of escape. But bare escape it seemed, for not a dozen feet behind her came her cavalier, white-flannelled, black-bearded, panting with laughter and pace. The pursuer was much younger than the pursued but that did not affect the ardor of the chase. The lady raced to the stairway leading to the running track above. Up she rushed, he after her. She reached the track and dashed around it, the ribbons of her belt standing straight out behind her. Her pursuer was visibly gaining. The gap narrowed. Nearer, nearer he drew, both hands outstretched to reach her waist."

At this point Sedgwick lost his nerve and, fearing they would spot him, slipped out an open window. "For me that race was forever lost and forever won," he later wrote. "The figures go flying motionless on the frieze of the Grecian urn: 'What men or Gods are these? What maidens loth? / What mad pursuit? What struggle to escape?'"

O N A N A U G U S T A F T E R N O O N in 1890, Isabella and Jack alighted from a train at Venice, assembled their masses of luggage on the quay, and went gliding in a fleet of gondolas up the Grand Canal to the Palazzo Barbaro. They had visited the palace six years earlier, when American friends had rented a floor. Isabella had been infatuated with the place, with its frescoed ceilings and marble-topped tables, its arches and inlaid floors. So the Gardners had rented the whole fantastic pile. Even Jack broke his laconic style to record their arrival. "Installed at Palazzo Barbaro. Hurrah!"

They rented the palace summer after summer. In the evenings they opened the tall French doors onto the Grand Canal, flooding the rooms with soft Venetian light. The Palazzo Barbaro, and Venice itself, expanded them, and the Gardners entered the great period of their collecting. In 1892, returning home through Paris, they bought James McNeill Whistler's *Harmony in Blue and Silver, Trouville*. While still in the French capital they heard that Vermeer's *The Concert* was coming up at auction. (Vermeer's pictures were still relatively unknown.) Isabella went to look at this painting and loved it. "Went to sale at Hotel Drouot," Jack's diary recorded. "Mrs. G bought the van der Meer for frs. 29,000." Two years later they bought Botticelli's *The Tragedy of Lucretia*, and two years after that, the famous picture that Rubens had called the best painting in the world, Titian's *The Rape of Europa*.

On December 10, 1898, at the age of sixty-one, Jack Gardner suffered an attack of apoplexy at the Exchange Club in Boston. He was carried home, and the doctors were summoned; he died at nine o'clock that night. Isabella's sorrow reduced her to a shadow in a week. She neither ate nor slept. Jack had supplied the steady counterpoint to Isabella's turbulence; her closest friends, remembering her terrible grief at the death of her son, worried that now, without Jack, she would be lost. They spoke of a nervous breakdown. But this was a different Isabella. Instead of withering away, she recovered, and resolved to complete the project she and Jack had conceived: to build a Palazzo Barbaro of their own, in Boston, as a public showcase for their art. Two weeks after Jack's death she summoned her architect, and the planning of Fenway Court began.

Battalions of workmen descended on the Fenway, a swath of reclaimed marshland a few miles from Beacon Hill. The main feature of the house would be its inner court—the facade of a Venetian palace facing inward, protected from the New England winter by an enormous canopy of glass. Isabella raked through Venice for whatever she could find. Eight complete balconies were stripped from houses on the Grand Canal. A sixteenth-century fireplace, four antique columns of peach-colored marble, Roman sarcophagi—it all went onto ships and sailed off to Boston.

Isabella Gardner was a nightmare client for Willard T. Sears, her architect. So vast were the rooms at Fenway Court that Boston's building inspectors quailed at the distance between supporting walls and wanted to cram the place with iron supporting columns. "She replied," wrote Sears, "that she would not have them and she did not care what they said." Sears worked out a compromise: a single iron column on the second floor. Isabella thought it would not be too bad; she could cover it in silk. So she agreed, but when it came time to put it up she stormed in and stopped the workmen. Sears led her patiently through it all again, and finally she consented to an iron column encased in wood. The architect had it put up instantly, before she could change her mind.

On November 18, 1901, with construction still under way, Isabella spent her first night at Fenway Court. The corridors had no proper floors, and Sears had to rush to get treads on the stairs. Isabella's biographer, Louise Hall Tharp, described the tumultuous state: "Now that the owner was a resident in her palace, the scene was right out of Lewis Carroll most of the time with Mrs. Gardner taking the part of the Red Queen and shouting 'Off with their heads' to all and sundry. But as in *Wonderland*, the condemned returned, more often than not, their heads still upon their shoulders. Gradually, she gathered about her people who not only managed to put up with her, but even liked her, temper tantrums and all."

On Christmas Eve, 1901, Reverend William B. Frisbie, rector of Boston's Church of the Advent, consecrated Isabella's private chapel in the Long Gallery on the third floor. Another year of hectic construction followed. Finally, the place was done and the art installed. The servants were presided over by a former gondolier named Theobaldo Travi, who had been a mason working at Fenway when Isabella met him. Something had sparked between them, and she made him her majordomo. "For the rest of her life," wrote Tharp, "he guarded her as he would have guarded a Venetian duchess. Joseph Lindon Smith designed a dress uniform for him—green knee breeches, crimson coat covered with gold braid, epaulets and Napoleonic hat of shining black. For this, he would have died for her, if he had not already committed his whole heart to her service."

Isabella had been dividing her time between Fenway and the residence on Beacon Street. At last she emptied the house she had shared with Jack of their most beloved possessions, installed them

Mrs. Gardner's House

in the palace, and moved in herself. In Boston, people nervously watched the mail for the most eagerly sought summons in New England: an invitation to the unveiling of Fenway Court. On January 1, 1903, at nine o'clock in the evening—"punctually," as she had stipulated—the street in front of the palazzo filled with carriages. In his eye-popping livery, Travi admitted the guests two by two. By candlelight they shed their coats, got into line, and climbed a sweeping staircase to greet their hostess. Isabella waited for them in a black gown. She wore her famous pearl rope and at her throat a ruby. In her hair sparkled a pair of diamonds: the twelve-carat "Rajah" and the twenty-five-carat "Light of India." Her guests came up and said hello and then went down again, by another flight, into the courtyard . . . to wait. When they were all assembled, and seated on small chairs, the majordomo raised his eyebrows at two footmen, who staggered onto the landing with a massive, gilded throne for Isabella. She settled herself, then nodded to the conductor of the Boston Symphony, and fifty musicians began to play.

I SABELLA STEWART GARDNER lived at Fenway Court for twenty-one years with one of the greatest private art collections in the world. There were paintings by Vermeer, Rembrandt, Velásquez, Titian; a pair of Botticellis and some French impressionists; as well as antique tapestries, plate, and statues. Sargent painted another portrait, *Mrs. Gardner in White*, in which the sitter gazed regally out, mistress of all she surveyed.

The Gardners had always intended to show their art to the public, and Isabella opened the doors of Fenway Court on February 23, 1903. Admission was one dollar. While she lived, Isabella saw to much of the administration and set herself to produce a blueprint for running it after her death. In a steady stream, the dicta poured

The Isabella Stewart Gardner Museum ca. 1925.
(Isabella Stewart Gardner Museum, Boston)

from her desk. "There shall be two women to live in the house on board wages and to be constantly on hand," she wrote. There would be "night and day watchmen—one for each time." The guards would be "young men whose business is ushering." Then came the strictest and most unyielding, and as events would prove, the most fateful, provision of all: the freezing of Fenway Court in time.

"If at any time the Trustees," she wrote, "shall place for exhibition in the Museum established under this my will any pictures or works of art other than such as I . . . own or have contracted for at my death, or if they shall at any time change the general disposition or arrangement of any articles . . . then I give the said land, Museum, pictures, statuary, works of art and bric-a-brac, furniture, books and papers . . . to the President and Fellows of Harvard Col-

Mrs. Gardner's House

lege in trust to sell . . . and to procure the dissolution of the Museum."

The trustees could not move a painting; they could not move a chair; they could not move a vase. Fenway Court and all it contained, exactly as it was, would be her final portrait. If anyone tampered with this legacy, "the President and Fellows of Harvard College" were directed to pack it all up and "sell the same in Paris, France." When Isabella died in 1924 at the age of eighty-four, she left behind a fantasy of self-aggrandizement conceived in the nineteenth century and handcuffed into place forever. Without the freedom to manage the collection, to rearrange it and secure it, and with the power of the endowment declining from inflation, the Gardner museum's administrators were helpless to keep their antiquated institution up to date. In security terms, the Gardner, like Russborough House six thousand miles away, was something of a tethered goat.

O N T H E E V E of March 17, 1990, the night before St. Patrick's Day, a young, part-time guard—a student—sat in the Gardner's cramped security office. He watched the closed-circuit monitors and listened to the rainfall drumming on the glass canopy above the courtyard. The courtyard itself was heaped with narcissus. The scent saturated the rooms, combining with the sound of pouring rain to spread a soporific atmosphere through the dark museum.

Just after one o'clock in the morning the doorbell rang at the side door at 2 Palace Road. Two men were standing there. They wore the uniform of the Boston police. Speaking into the intercom, they told the guard they had been dispatched to investigate a report of a disturbance at the museum. The guard released the lock, and the men went in.

A security counter separated the two men from the guard, who at this point was still within reach of the master alarm. "You look familiar," one of the phony police officers then said. "I think we have a warrant for you. Let me see your I.D." The guard summoned his partner, patrolling elsewhere in the building, then stepped from behind the counter. As he did, he removed himself from proximity to the main alarm and lost his only chance to alert the outside world to what was happening at the Gardner. The second security guard, also a young part-timer, soon arrived, whereupon the two "policemen" grabbed them and overpowered them. They handcuffed the guards, led them to the basement, and tied them to utility pipes. They wrapped the young men's faces in duct tape, leaving only their noses free.

When the thieves returned upstairs, they attempted to dismantle the internal surveillance system. They ripped the wires from the closed-circuit camera and destroyed the tape. They tried to disable the system that controlled sensors throughout the museum, but succeeded only in disconnecting its line to a printer. The sensors, which laced the rooms and hallways of the Gardner with a web of invisible infrared beams, continued to feed data to the museum's central computer. That is how we know the route the robbers took as they went through Mrs. Gardner's house and pulled off, as the figures would later show, the biggest robbery in American history.

They went to the Dutch Room on the second floor and tackled Rembrandt's *The Storm on the Sea of Galilee*. The picture hung from long wires, and they had to give it a hard tug. They dropped it as it came away, leaving a little heap of paint and varnish chips on the floor. The two then smashed the glass on Vermeer's *The Concert* and Govaert Flinck's *Landscape with an Obelisk* and pulled out the canvases. They took down *A Lady and Gentleman in Black*, formerly attributed to Rembrandt. At the exit from the Dutch Room they yanked down the Rembrandt self-portrait but left it on the floor.

The thieves split up. One of them went downstairs with the art. The other went off alone, tripping the Gardner's infrared beams all

Mrs. Gardner's House

the way. He tore a set of Degas prints from a wooden partition and returned to the ground floor. In the Blue Room beside the public entrance, they yanked Manet's *Chez Tortoni* from the bolts that held it to the wall. Two hours after they had come, they left with thirteen works.

The theft was discovered at seven-thirty that morning, when another guard and a janitor arrived at the entrance at 2 Palace Road, buzzed, got no answer, and called the supervisor. They found the night guards trussed in the basement. Within hours the Boston city police, Massachusetts State Police, and the FBI had the place packed with crime-scene investigators. The only thing that came out of the Gardner faster than fingerprints was theories.

Boston's newspaper readers were soon learning that the thefts had likely been commissioned by a South American or Japanese collector. This conjecture became known as the "Dr. No theory," after one of spy-writer Ian Fleming's larger-than-life villains. Other experts told reporters that they thought the pictures would be ransomed back to the museum's insurers. This was never a possibility: Like many museums, the Gardner had no theft insurance, the premiums being prohibitive. The story then became that the museum itself would have to pay, and in fact the Gardner quickly offered one million dollars for information leading to the return of the works.

Two months after the robbery, a story in the *Boston Globe* claimed that police had "targeted" some dozen criminals "scattered across the world." One got the impression of the long arm of the law, reaching out for the evildoers. "As details begin to emerge about the two-month probe," the reporter wrote, "law enforcement sources said that the suspects' movements were under close scrutiny by federal agents, including one suspect who was under surveillance during a recent arrival at [Boston's] Logan Airport."

It was all baloney. The FBI had nothing. Their files listed the robbers as Unknown Suspect Number One and Unknown Suspect Number Two, and therein lay the tale. The guards told detectives they thought the men had been in their early thirties. The first was short, with short black hair and a narrow face and square-shaped gold frame glasses; the second was just over six feet, a little heavier, and with hair that fell to his collar. Each wore a shiny black mustache and identical clothing—described by the FBI as "fully ornamented dark blue police uniform and hat, and dark shoes, with patch on left shoulder, possibly with wording 'Boston Police'"—and carried a black, police-style radio clipped to his belt. In other words, most of what the investigators knew of the robbers' appearance were physical details that the criminals would have jettisoned immediately.

Theories rose and fell. The fact that the thieves had taken a Chinese vase and a Napoleonic finial but left behind a Titian and a Velásquez was cited as proof that they were amateurs, thieves but not *art* thieves. Others maintained that such apparent randomness meant exactly the opposite: that the thieves were consummate professionals, gathering only those objects specified by contract.

The value of the thirteen works stolen from the Gardner museum was put at two hundred million dollars. This figure later climbed to three hundred million dollars. Supporting the astronomic sum, almost by itself, was the Vermeer. Of thirty-six Vermeers known to exist, two were now missing.

Investigators found a suspect. Ten years earlier, Brian McDevitt had gone to jail for a bungled art theft in upstate New York. He and an accomplice had hijacked a Federal Express truck, subdued the driver with ether, and, wearing the company's livery, had driven off to the Hyde Collection Art Museum in Glens Falls. An essential tactical ingredient of their plan had been ease of entry, and when they arrived at the target to find it had just closed, they abandoned their scheme. The truck driver later identified McDevitt.

Because McDevitt's crime had involved art, and he had worn a uniform as a disguise, the FBI computer spat him out as a Gardner match, and the agents put him on their list. McDevitt, a native of Swampscott, a suburb northeast of Boston, had moved back to Boston after his short spell in jail for the failed Glens Falls job, and lived in the Boston area at the time of the 1990 Gardner robbery. He had since moved to Los Angeles and set himself up as a screenwriter, claiming a distinguished writing past. The FBI's interest in him as a suspect quickened in the fall of 1991, a year and a half after the robbery, when McDevitt pitched a screenplay about an art theft. In the prospective film, the thieves cached their booty in a cave in Germany. Instead of explaining his plot to a producer, McDevitt got the chance to tell it to a grand jury. In the end the FBI decided that McDevitt, foiled by a locked door in his only previous art crime, was not the mastermind behind the Gardner theft. With McDevitt cleared, they concentrated on another suspect, Myles Connor.

The name of Myles Connor, Jr., came up early in the investigation, and it is easy to see why. He was a famous Massachusetts felon with a taste for stealing art. Connor was in prison at the time of the Gardner robbery, but detectives in Boston thought he might have planned and directed the crime. A few months after the Gardner job Connor appeared for sentencing on a string of convictions that included art theft. The federal court judge called him "rotten to the core" and gave him twenty years—twice what the prosecutor had asked for.

Connor's lawyer loftily dismissed the suggestion that his client had masterminded the Gardner theft. "Myles would never tolerate butchering art," he said, referring to the rough treatment of the Gardner pictures at the bandits' hands. Whatever informa-

Myles Connor Jr., as he appeared in "The Myles Connor 1950s Rock & Roll Revue." (From the collection of Myles Connor)

tion Connor had went with him into a federal penitentiary—for a while.

IN THE 1950S Connor had climbed to fame with his rock-and-roll band, Myles Connor and the Wild Ones. They played across New England, headlining above such rising bands as the Beach Boys. O'Connor called himself the President of Rock. This life, by itself, seems not to have met his deepest needs, and by and by he drifted into his true métier—crime.

In 1965 police caught him coming out of a house on the Maine coast with an armload of Tiffany lamps. The sheriff's deputy, a sixty-year-old veteran, knew Connor, whose family had vacationed nearby. He tried to talk Connor into surrendering. Instead, Connor tossed him down a hill, fired a shot, and fled. The police caught him at a roadblock and locked him up. Connor broke out of jail with a cake of soap carved into the shape of a pistol.

The Maine police recaptured him, partly with the help of his mother, who appeared in a police car and, using a megaphone, begged him to surrender. Said Connor: "It was damned embarrassing." He spent a few months in jail, got out in early 1966, and by April the Massachusetts State Police went looking for him in connection with a plot to steal a Rembrandt from Harvard University's Fogg Art Museum. When they raided Connor's apartment in suburban Revere, police found seven swords missing from the Peabody Museum in Salem, Massachusetts, and antique Chinese objects stolen from the Forbes Museum in Milton. The police caught up with Connor on April 27. He shot one of them and in the ensuing firefight took four bullets himself. The gun battle raged through the alleys of Boston's Back Bay until, following a trail of blood, the police cornered Connor on a rooftop. They handcuffed him and shackled his legs and battered him.

Connor got out of prison six years later. Two years after that, in 1974, he went to the Maine estate of the Woolworth family and took three paintings by N. C. Wyeth and one by Andrew Wyeth. The police had Connor as their suspect from the beginning and caught him at Mashpee, on Cape Cod, trying to fence the pictures. Because he had been in prison for felonies, the new crime, a felony, meant that Connor faced a long sentence. While out on bail, he drove to the Boston Museum of Fine Arts with two accomplices, went inside, and snatched Rembrandt's *Portrait of Elsbeth van Rijn* from the wall. "I was out of there in six seconds flat. My two guys had guns—a machine gun and a pistol. The guy with the machine gun fired a burst and the guards threw themselves flat. Except this one guard—an old Polish retired cop. He wouldn't give up but kept after me right to the van and—can you believe it?—was actually hanging to my leg! I had to hit him on the head."

In a plea bargain, Connor traded the Rembrandt for a suspended sentence on the Woolworth theft, but by 1975 was back inside a Massachusetts jail, imprisoned on a variety of charges, including murder. Paroled in 1986, he enjoyed three years of what one reporter called his "criminal prime," garnering large sums of cash by robbing drug dealers. This spree came to an end in November 1989, when Connor pled guilty to the theft of a pair of seventeenth-century Dutch paintings worth four hundred thousand dollars from the Mead Art Museum at Amherst College, Massachusetts, and went back to jail. A month later, a visitor smuggled in four hacksaw blades hidden in a book, and Connor tried to saw his way to freedom. He was caught, and the next year, 1990, a federal judge in Springfield, Illinois, weighing all this in the balance alongside a batch of new drug and weapons charges, sentenced him to the twenty years.

He was seven years into the stretch when, on August 13, 1997, a petty crook named William P. Youngworth III, about to be arraigned on drug and gun charges, stepped in front of a television camera on the courthouse steps in Dedham, a town south of Boston, and said he could get the Gardner pictures back if the authorities met three demands: pay him the reward (it had just been raised to five million dollars); grant him immunity from prosecution; and release Myles Connor.

The demands drew hearty laughs all around, except from Tom Mashberg, a crime reporter for the *Boston Herald*. Five days after the courthouse manifesto, Mashberg got into a Ford Crown Victoria with a delegate of Youngworth's and rode about an hour out of Boston. At one o'clock in the morning they pulled up in front of a warehouse in a run-down district. A woman hurried over to the car. "Billy sent us," said the driver.

Mrs. Gardner's House

Mashberg followed his guide into the building. With a flashlight to illuminate their path, they picked their way through the darkness and up four flights of stairs. In a corridor lined with steel doors Mashberg's companion stopped at one, pulled out some keys, and opened a padlock. They stepped inside. Wearing rubber gloves, the man extracted a cardboard picture tube from a bin and tugged out the rolled-up canvas. "It was, I am certain, Rembrandt's *The Storm on the Sea of Galilee*," Mashberg later wrote, "arguably the most famous missing painting in the world. I saw frayed edges, where the painting had been cut from its frame on the night it was stolen, and I was shown, in the flashlight's beam, Rembrandt's signature."

Mashberg called his story an "international sensation" and sold it to *Vanity Fair*. He brokered a meeting between representatives of Youngworth, Connor, the Gardner, and the FBI. Youngworth had given Mashberg some paint chips, and the reporter secured the opinion of an old-paint-chip expert from Chicago, who verified that the chips were indeed old paint, and Dutch. "His [the paint-chip expert's] findings produced headlines everywhere," Mashberg wrote. Except at the Gardner, where they provoked skepticism.

The Connor-Youngworth episode petered out into rancor. It seems that Youngworth had been Connor's trustee, his responsibility being to care for Connor's possessions. For a man locked up most of his life, Connor had put together a substantial hoard. It included not only valuable samurai swords, a weakness of Connor's, but other art and antiques too. Alas for Connor, Youngworth was a drug addict; inevitably, he sold some of Connor's things. When Connor discovered this, as apparently he did in the course of Mashberg's investigation, he severed his connection to Youngworth. Connor's only benefit from this bizarre stunt was a move from the Illinois prison to a penitentiary in his native state, a transfer effected by Donald Stern, the U.S. attorney for Massachusetts, who had decided, as a result of Mashberg's machinations, to quiz Connor about the Gardner robbery. "I concluded he had nothing worth trading," Stern said later, "so he finished his sentence."

STUDENTS OF ART THEFT nurse the belief that the Gardner robbery was connected to Cahill's theft at Russborough. A mass of circumstance has encouraged this view. American Irish support for the IRA, for example, necessarily enlisted a criminal participation: It takes criminals to launder money and buy illegal arms. Since the IRA had to operate in the criminal theater, other criminal connections flowed from this, and "Boston Irish" gangsters had close ties to their Dublin counterparts. The North Atlantic is a sort of underworld Irish Sea, with Canada, the United States, and Ireland laced together by the criminal trade. When Montreal police were staking out that city's Irish mob, the West End Gang, suspected of snatching a Goya from the Basilica in Quebec City, they stumbled upon paintings stolen from Dunsany Castle in County Meath, allegedly by the IRA. In a feature on the Gardner theft, *Time* reported that "an IRA operative was gunned down shortly after bragging to an ex–FBI agent that he had information on a major art theft." Connor himself, in Boston, bragged about stealing art to support "the cause"—the armed struggle to unify Ireland. Moreover, because the Gardner robbers had taken a Vermeer, while leaving behind the Titian, the Botticellis, and the Velásquez, investigators naturally wondered whether the Boston hit had been inspired by Russborough. Kevin Cullen of the *Boston Globe,* who has written extensively on the criminal links between Ireland and the United States, believes that imitation might easily have played a role. "These guys follow each other's exploits," he said, "the way some people follow baseball."

With all this in mind I decided to go and talk to Myles Connor. He had served eleven years of his twenty-year sentence and was now out on parole. I opened negotiations with his gatekeeper, a sometime music promoter named Al Dotoli. "What's in it for Myles?" he said.

"I don't know," I told him. "How about two hundred and fifty dollars?"

"It would have to be cash."

"Yes," I said, and on a bright blue day in May 2002, I flew into Boston and rented a car and drove south on Interstate 93 to the Neponset-Quincy exit, then crossed the bridge that leads to the ocean. In my breast pocket was a neat little wad of bills. The sea sparkled with light, and a breeze blew off the water. I parked at a shoreside restaurant and went inside. Three men were waiting for me in the lobby: Dotoli, a big guy named Scott Anderson, and Connor.

Connor had abandoned the bearded, rakish look I had seen in photographs. At the brink of sixty, he was clean-shaven and dressed in a pale golf shirt and beige chinos. A member of Mensa, an organization for people with high IQs, he speaks well and sometimes extravagantly, using words like *fiendish* and *egregious* to describe the long campaign of police harassment he has had to endure for no better reason than that he has ripped people off and assaulted them. He was once convicted of murdering two young women by driving screwdrivers into their heads but was acquitted on retrial.

They told me to leave my car in the parking lot and get into their van, Connor and me in the backseat. We commenced a twenty-minute drive through Quincy. We followed a tortuous route, winding here and there until I couldn't tell where we were headed. It didn't seem the right time to start the interview, so I just handed Connor the two hundred and fifty dollars. "Thanks," he said, and we continued in silence. I confess that I started to dwell on the screwdriver-in-the-head story, which I had read for the first time in the plane on the way to Boston, in old newspaper stories downloaded from the Internet. Dotoli's reflection in the driving mirror, sunglasses hiding his eyes, looked more sinister with every turn we took. But instead of taking me down to the beach and hacking me to bits and leaving me for the crabs, they stopped at a restaurant and we all got out and went inside.

Connor studied the menu very carefully and ordered grilled scallops in a ginger sauce. He asked for mineral water. Dotoli had a martini and a steak. I forget what Anderson asked for, but he seemed to enjoy it; after all, the meal was on me. "Two-fifty *plus* the lunch," Dotoli explained.

We spent an hour talking about cars Connor had owned, including a dark blue Griffith. The Griffith was a limited-edition powerhouse produced between 1963 and 1967, about three hundred cars in all, styled with a savage grace and sent off racing down the freeway with a 450-horsepower engine and a speedometer that stopped at 160 mph. Connor claims to have driven from Northampton to Quincy, a distance of ninety miles, in forty minutes flat. It's quite possible he did, because he said he liked to run the tolls for fun, to see if he could get a trooper to come after him.

We finished lunch and went to Dotoli's to watch a tape of a 1998 ABC television news feature about Connor, hosted by Forest Sawyer. It began with a lot of footage of Connor in his cell, waving his arms around and making karate cuts in the air and kicking out at a spot on the wall. The narration described him as a martial-arts expert. Then they got down to the meat of the interview, in which Connor claimed to know the exact location of the Gardner pictures.

"They're close to Boston?" Sawyer asked.

"Yes," said Connor.

"And you could get them back in an hour?"

"Forty minutes."

Connor had since suffered a heart attack that temporarily cut off oxygen to his brain, slightly impairing his speech and removing exactly that part of his memory that contained the whereabouts of the Gardner pictures.

"You mean," I said, "now you don't know where they are?"

"That's right."

"You did, but don't."

"Exactly."

"So you can't say whether they are forty minutes away or, say, in a cellar in Dublin."

"No."

"I'm not saying I think they *are* in Dublin," I said.

"No," he said, "and I'm not saying I think they aren't."

I put away my notebook, and we shook hands all around. They gave me a dub of the ABC tape, a glossy publicity shot of Connor from his rocker days, and a copy of the welcoming letter from American Mensa Ltd. They took me back to my car, and I posed for a snapshot with Connor. Before I got in my car I said to Connor, "What about Whitey Bulger?"

"What about him?"

"Some people think he was behind the Gardner thing."

"They think he was behind everything."

"Well, he sort of was."

"If you say so."

A T THE TIME of the Gardner robbery James "Whitey" Bulger was the top Irish-American criminal in Boston. He led the Winter Hill Mob. In 1994 federal prosecutors, at secret grand-jury proceedings, obtained indictments against him under the Racketeering Influenced and Corrupt Organizations (RICO) statute, for eighteen counts of murder, conspiracy to commit murder, conspiracy to commit extortion, narcotics distribution, and money laundering. Tipped off to the indictments, Bulger vanished. The FBI put him on the Ten Most Wanted list and started to look for the tipster.

They found him in their own ranks. John J. Connolly, Jr., an FBI special agent, had grown up on the same South Boston street as Bulger. They had remained friends and had entered, although on opposing sides, what is after all the same business—crime. When Connolly's assignment became the penetration of organized crime, he enlisted Bulger as an informant. At first it was a straightforward arrangement, known to Connolly's superiors at the FBI: In return for Bulger's regular betrayals of other criminals, he was more or less left alone. In time this commerce, inherently corrupt, corrupted Connolly, and he began accepting money from Bulger.

Connolly went on trial in the U.S. District Court in Boston in 2002, where a jury convicted him of racketeering and taking bribes. Facing prison, Connolly could have been expected to trade information about Bulger in order to lighten the sentence that he faced. One such item of information might have been the whereabouts of the Gardner pictures, since it was likely that Bulger, the most powerful criminal in Boston when the art was stolen, either would have stolen it himself or would have known who had.

Connolly got ten years, which suggests that if he knew anything about the Gardner thefts, he did not trade it. Charley Hill, for one, thought the Connolly trial was the best chance to break the case. Hill's involvement with the Russborough investigation, and his experience with art crime generally as a Scotland Yard detective, had led him to suspect a Bulger connection. "My personal view," he said, "is that it [the Gardner robbery] was done for money and a favor, and in retirement of a debt," and that Bulger was connected to it. He would say no more.

Dick Ellis, too, believed in a Bulger connection. According to Ellis, an English criminal informant, code-named Turbo, was approached at an antiques fair in Miami in 1995 by a known handler

Mrs. Gardner's House

of stolen property. The man said that a Boston criminal, Patrick Nee, had offered him all the Gardner property for ten million dollars. Nee was an associate of Bulger's. Turbo relayed the information to Ellis, and Ellis passed it on, first to the Boston field office of the FBI and later to Larry Potts, a former deputy director of the FBI, who had been retained by the Gardner to retrieve its art. At the time of this writing, Potts had not had much luck finding the Gardner art. An attempt to gain the help of William P. Youngworth III had brought the following written response from Youngworth: "Yes, I would be delighted to help you and the Gardner Museum recover their former property. Kindly remit 50 million dollars U.S. and a signed immunity agreement issued by the Attorney General of the United States."

C ONNECTIONS BETWEEN the Russborough and Gardner thefts are tantalizing, if speculative. The crimes took place on a shared criminal terrain with historical links. What is certain is that the 1990 Gardner robbery pushed up the notional value of a Vermeer, leading to estimates first of two hundred million dollars, and then three hundred million dollars, for the Gardner art, with the Vermeer accounting for the lion's share. There can be no doubt that this raised the stakes for Cahill, and his gang must have renewed their demands that he try to move the Russborough art. When he did, a soft-spoken Irish policeman named Liam Hogan heard about it. Hogan had been watching for exactly such a sign.

{ 8 }

Liam's Game

LIAM HOGAN'S first exposure to the Russborough story came in 1974, when his father, Ned Hogan, was commanding the Garda in west Cork. Hogan senior was the man who sent his constables fanning out into the remote peninsulas and caught Rose Dugdale. Ned Hogan got the Beit collection back in a week. When Liam Hogan took over the Russborough investigation in 1992, the pictures had been gone six years.

By the time I met him in January 2002, Hogan had become a detective in the Garda's secretive Special Branch. He is of average height and weight, with a thatch of curly, light-brown hair and a gray, unblinking gaze. You might not notice this if you walked by, because you might not notice Hogan. He has a talent for observing without being observed.

Our appointment was for two-thirty in the afternoon in the lobby bar of Dublin's Westbury Hotel. I had his description, down to the coat he would be wearing: tweed, herringbone, black and white. I came out of the elevator ten minutes early and stood where the marble staircase comes up from the ground floor into

Liam Hogan
(Pat Shelly,
An Garda Síochána)

the hotel's reception area. As prosperous Dubliners bustled in from the high-end shops on Grafton Street, I scrutinized them one by one. I searched the lobby. There was not a trace of Hogan. Not until I decided to move on into the bar myself to wait for him did I see him, when he seemingly detached himself from thin air and suddenly appeared beside me. We shook hands and sat down to discuss the long frustrations of the Garda in its pursuit of the Russborough haul, and how Hogan had come to make the mission his own.

He was born in 1949, the first of six children of Ned and Eileen Hogan. The family lived in a semidetached bungalow on Pouladuff Road in a suburb of Cork. Ned was then a detective inspector in the Garda division that formed the Cork city police. There were four detective inspectors in the whole of Ireland: two in Dublin, one in Shannon, and Ned. "He was a very friendly character," said Liam Hogan. "People liked him, even the criminals."

Hogan was keenly aware of his father's work. In the 1950s and 1960s Irish police spent much of their time tracking the IRA. Ned worked long hours, often going an entire month without two days off in a row. The front parlor of the Hogans' house became an informal police station. "He was in there all hours of the day and night," recalled Liam Hogan. "It was a no-go area for the kids. Victims would come to see him there, and criminals too, obviously facing jail and looking for a deal. You'd hear him talking in there, and wonder who it was."

Sometimes Ned's picture appeared in the paper. He had status in the community—local hero, confessor, pillar. Liam admired him above everyone, and when he reached the age of twenty-one he got in a car with his father and drove sixty miles north to Templemore, in County Tipperary, where they turned through the gates of the Garda training college, said good-bye, and Liam stepped into the life he had wanted since boyhood. "Ah, it was a great place. There were only twenty-three of us in that intake, from the whole country, so you were lucky to get in."

At the end of his training, Hogan's superiors asked him where he'd like to work, and he said anywhere but Dublin. "I thought it'd be too tough, and I told them, and I finished up in Limerick, which you couldn't find a tougher place. Dublin hadn't a patch on it. We used to call it stab city. There wasn't a night that you wouldn't end up with a prisoner."

The city of Limerick lies on the River Shannon, a few miles above the point where the river opens out into a series of long, estuarine bays that take it down to the Atlantic. Swans glide beneath the city bridges. The cathedral church of St. Mary, raised in 1172 by the last king of Munster, displays the finest wooden carvings that survive

Liam's Game

from ancient Catholic Ireland. St. Mary's is the fortress church of King John's Castle, a thirteenth-century defensive block of gray stone whose northern wall runs two hundred feet along the southern bank of the Shannon. The castle still bears the scars of the Protestant cannon that bombarded it in 1691, when the Catholic army of James Stuart drew its line at the river and faced the Williamite forces that had routed it on the Boyne. The defense crumbled, and Ireland fell to the prince of Orange, and the struggle to reverse that moment has not ceased.

The most famous creature of that struggle has been the IRA. But the roots of insurrection stretch much farther back in time, into an ancient tradition of secret, peasant societies formed by the dispossessed Gaels in the centuries following the Norman invasion, and persisting into later times. These small, clandestine bands had no chance of reversing history. Their mission was to exact a steady taxation of terror from those in power over them. They depended for concealment on the complicity of their fellow Irishmen, who shared their language, race, and fate. This old tradition of resistance to authority was too deeply ingrained to evaporate with Irish independence, and the job of a policeman in Ireland is always at war with the past.

I N 1979, after eight years in uniform in Limerick, Liam Hogan went into plain clothes and transferred to the murder squad in Dublin. At the time, the unit's strength was only nine. Based at the Jones's Road Garda station, the murder squad covered the whole country. Not long after Hogan arrived, the IRA assassinated Earl Mountbatten, the uncle of Prince Philip, Queen Elizabeth's consort, blowing up his thirty-foot pleasure boat as he sailed in Donegal Bay. The fifty-pound bomb reduced the craft to splinters, killing not only the earl but also his fourteen-year-old grandson, a woman relative, and a fifteen-year-old boatboy from Enniskillen. Mountbatten was a war hero, much loved by the British royal family. He had held the title first sea lord, was the last viceroy of India, and is said to have been more of a father to the present Prince of Wales than Prince Philip himself. London had barely had time to digest the atrocity when another IRA bomb went off. The massive device had been planted by a road that ran along the northern shore of Carlingford Lough, the sea-bay that separates County Down in Northern Ireland from County Louth in the republic. Two truck-loads of British paratroopers had been making their way along the road when the device was triggered, and six soldiers died instantly. Their wounded comrades immediately came under sniper fire from across the lough. Desperate, they radioed for help, and an army helicopter arrived with reinforcements and landed in a nearby field. It was a trap. The IRA detonated a second bomb, killing twelve more soldiers and wounding twenty.

The assassination of Mountbatten and the ambush on the border coincided with a general escalation of criminal activity in Ireland. With the police engaged on many fronts, and the criminal milieu enriched by weaponry flowing into the country to the IRA, the government expanded the Garda by one thousand men, or roughly 10 percent, to its present level of about eleven thousand. The murder squad became the serious-crime investigation unit and moved from Jones's Road to Phoenix Park. Hogan found himself exactly where he had not wanted to be, squarely in the midst of Ireland's most robust criminal activity. It was a far cry from the image of the policeman as the friend of the community, meting out justice in the front parlor. Twice Hogan applied for a transfer to Cork, but he was turned down.

In 1988 the serious-crime branch was reorganized into the central detective unit and moved to the Harcourt Square complex. This move brought Hogan into the domain of Noel Conroy, one

Liam's Game

of the masterminds of the Tango squad, which was then only a year old and still in the full cry of harassing Cahill. The huntsman's horn was sounding on the hill then, when Hogan began the long stalk that was to put him on the heels of Cahill.

"I had a theory that if you went out between one and two o'clock in the afternoon," he said, "and drove into the flats [public-housing areas], the people there wouldn't expect to see you, because usually we went at night, and so maybe we could grab someone we'd been looking for."

On one such visit Hogan spotted a late-model Mercedes-Benz, not the kind of vehicle normally found in the flats. Hogan wrote down the license number. When he checked it later, he found that the car had not been stolen, but noticed that the owner had recently reported a burglary at his house involving art. He thought that the man might have visited the flats in answer to a ransom demand. He was right.

The victim had appeared on the British edition of the *Antiques Roadshow* television program with one of his paintings: a picture by Sir John Lavery. Lavery was a well-known figure in twentieth-century Irish art. His portrait of his American wife, Hazel, decorated Ireland's paper currency. The Garda contacted the victim, who was instructed not to pay the ransom. Hogan tapped the phone of a Dublin art forger he thought might be involved. When the forger booked a flight to Cardiff, Wales, Hogan tipped off Scotland Yard. The forger flew into Wales, retrieved three stolen paintings he had shipped ahead, and the police caught him cold.

It was not possible to solve an art crime in Ireland in 1988 without the Russborough thefts echoing in the background. Hogan's success confirmed a number of suspicions: that stolen art could be marketed abroad, and that even low-level criminals had foreign contacts. When Hogan moved to an anticorruption unit based at

Phoenix Park, he carried these thoughts with him. Russborough had settled in his mind.

In 1990 Hogan was promoted to detective sergeant. That same year, Noel Conroy moved from Harcourt Square to Phoenix Park to head up, as a chief superintendent, a crime and security unit. When the Garda decided soon after to reconstitute the serious-crime investigation unit, with Conroy at its head, Hogan joined it. His assignment was antiracketeering; his reason for taking the post was Conroy. "I had built up a relationship," Hogan says, "so I stayed with him when we moved. I liked his style of work and operation. You could explore ideas with Conroy—you'd value his judgment and guidance."

Hogan's antiracketeering work gave him a view into the higher criminal activity of Ireland. He came to understand that the methods available to tax cheats and fraud artists and drug barons for laundering money had also become available, by criminal osmosis, to the wider underworld.

The Tango squad's surveillance of Cahill was no longer as relentless as it had been, and Cahill had opportunities to explore ways to dispose of his assets and collect the proceeds.

By 1992, with the three-hundred-million-dollar valuation of the Gardner pictures fresh in his mind, Cahill decided to reach outside Ireland into the larger criminal marketplace to dispose of the picture. The Garda had an important snout close to Cahill: Tommy Coyle. Through Coyle and other sources, Hogan learned that Cahill was opening another bid to move the Beit collection, and that it was to be offshore. "So I went to Conroy with the information and laid it all out and said, 'Let's do a sting,' and he supported that."

HOGAN MOVED INTO a separate location at Phoenix Park. The quarters he took consisted of a single room, with a direct outside line. Nothing on the door identified his purpose, and if anyone asked, he brushed them off with a vague reply. In effect, he established a unit of two: himself and Conroy. He reported to no one else, and no one else knew exactly what he was doing. "I wanted to keep it tight at the time," he said. "An operation like that—you have to be fierce tight." Conroy arranged a wiretap on the subject Hogan had identified: a genial Dublin rogue named Niall Mulvihill. Mulvihill had approached Cahill with an offer to help broker the sale of the Beit pictures. Cahill, with his own deep contacts, had already settled on a buyer. Mulvihill fished around for an agent to transfer the works and found one in England.

Six years had passed since the Russborough raid, and two since the sole Garda success—the recovery of one of the Metsus in Istanbul. Yet the pictures had not passed entirely from the radar screen. In the wake of the Turkish operation, a steady snow of blips told police that Cahill was anxious to unload the paintings. At Scotland Yard, Dick Ellis later recalled, the tips flowed in so regularly that detectives would say, "If it's the Beit pictures, it must be Friday." Informants sometimes provided proof that the pictures really were in play, such as a photograph of a painting against a current newspaper.

About the time that Liam Hogan began to monitor Mulvihill, Ellis got a call from a detective in Leighton Buzzard, Bedfordshire. The detective had a mole inside an Irish gang operating in the area. The source said the Beit collection was about to move.

In Dublin, Hogan had the same information. He had informants, too, and the wiretap on Mulvihill. As soon as Mulvihill made the English contact, Hogan called Scotland Yard and got Ellis. With this connection—Hogan and Ellis—a brisk exchange of intelligence went back and forth across the Irish Sea. This exchange would not have taken place a year before, because it depended on a single development: Hogan.

As in any service that lives by intelligence, the security of that

Lady Writing a Letter with Her Maid *by Johannes Vermeer*
(Courtesy of The National Gallery of Ireland)

Isabella Stewart Gardner *by John Singer Sargent*
(Isabella Stewart Gardner Museum, Boston,
Massachusetts, USA/Bridgeman Art Library)

For years, Jørgen Wadum, chief conservator of the Mauritshuis museum at The Hague,
had searched for an explanation of how Vermeer had achieved his amazingly convincing perspectives.
Finally, in a basement room in Antwerp, almost by accident, Wadum found a pinhole dead in the center
of the left eye of the seated woman in Lady Writing a Letter with Her Maid, and made the
breakthrough discovery, described in chapter 9, of the painter's maddeningly simple technique.
(Courtesy of The National Gallery of Ireland)

The Scream, *1893 by Edvard Munch (Photo by J. Lathion; courtesy of the National Gallery, Norway/Artists Rights Society, New York)*

intelligence was a preoccupation of Scotland Yard. In 1992, the Yard's dectectives thought they had a problem. The succession of tips about the Beit pictures, backed by such credible evidence as the photographs, had failed to lead anywhere. Ellis and his superiors had naturally worked with the Garda on some of the tips. As investigation after investigation sailed into a windless sea, they became convinced that the problem lay in Ireland: Cahill had penetrated the Garda's operations. Someone, Ellis believed, was leaking back to Cahill the tips that had come from his own gang. This compromised not only the operations of police who would act on the tips but the tipsters too, since Cahill could reason backward to the source. To plug these leaks, the Art and Antiques squad had stopped talking to the Garda. Liam Hogan's operation, with its single need-to-know superior—Conroy—persuaded the Yard to deal with Phoenix Park again. Said Ellis of Hogan, "We trusted him."

As Cahill launched his final bid to move the Beit collection then, an array of intelligence sources was deployed against him. Most of these were informants. The British had at least four sources inside Irish groups in England, and the Garda had Dublin teeming with snouts. Some of these were paid informers; others gave information in exchange for favors from police, such as not being put in jail.

The problem with informants is that much of what they say is false. Sometimes their own sources have lied to them, or they themselves have originated the lie. There are several reasons for this mendacity. For example, the informant may not know anything about a particular crime or criminal, and be inventing a tale only to have something to sell. Information is a commodity, and he is a supplier. His customer, the policeman, either cannot know if the information is true or false, or, if he does know, cannot know if the informer is passing it to him knowingly. In these circumstances, there is not much risk in lying, and something to gain.

Liam's Game

In the case of an informant passing on a lie he believes to be true, the lie may have been planted by a criminal to confuse police. After all, criminals understand the treacherous nature of their own milieu and how to use it to advantage. Cahill's obsession with loyalty was no more than the sensible practice of a man determined to preserve the security of his operations in a leaky world. A natural extension of that concern is feeding out false leads.

The investigator seeking to interdict a criminal operation is therefore often working in a fog of lies, and while Hogan and Ellis knew for certain as early as 1992 that the paintings were again in play, they did not know that the game would get under way on a June night in 1993, when the last of the pictures came down out of the Wicklow Mountains to a house in Tallaght. The Vermeer and the Goya were already there, and had been in Dublin since the failed sting of 1987, transported here and there about the city in time to Cahill's regular spasms of paranoia. Now the gang assembled the haul, wrapped the paintings carefully one by one in quilted blankets, and secreted them in the false bottom of a truck. They drove to Dun Laoghaire and onto the late-night ferry to Wales. In the early morning they docked at Holyhead, and the Beit collection rumbled down the ramp and onto the soil it had left forty-one years earlier, except this time it was not with its owner.

Let us assume a straightforward route: The truck sped eastward through the Marches into Gloucestershire and made its way toward the British capital. Late that afternoon or, if the traffic was heavy, in the evening, the cargo arrived at the fenced compound of an Irish-born north London car dealer, and the gate swung shut behind it.

The first Ellis knew of the pictures' arrival in England came from one of those sudden gusts of traitorous wind that bedevil the criminal world. The Irish gang in Leighton Buzzard, hearing about the paintings, staged a raid and got away with most of Cahill's loot.

Probably the London car dealer himself, or even Mulvihill, engineered the operation, simply to increase their take. In any event, the mole inside the gang alerted Ellis, who moved swiftly to recover what he could.

"We carried out a wide sweep against a number of targets," Ellis explained, "some of them unrelated to the art. There were six of us from Art and Antiques and a dozen guys from the Regional Crime squad. We wanted them to think it was a general sweep against known criminals, and that whatever we found was a matter of luck, not a tip."

They found the Rubens *Portrait of a Dominican Monk* stuffed behind a sofa in a flat in the London quarter of Maida Vale. One painting was plucked from a locker at Euston Station. Four other pictures were hidden in a factory in Bedfordshire that manufactured oil paintings. "There were thousands of paintings in the place," said Ellis, "racks and racks of them, and the gang had slipped the stolen art in among them. We spent the better part of a night searching the place. We told them we were looking for drugs."

The car dealer, possibly to protect himself from Cahill's suspicion, had managed to "save" four of the paintings. Unknown to Ellis, these were headed for the Continent—as before, in the false bottom of a truck.

THE TRUCK WENT BY FERRY from Dover to the Belgian port of Ostende. From the coast, the paintings came east to Antwerp, in Vermeer's time a great trading city, but now a rather dowdy town on the flat, gray river-plain of Belgium. The only sparkle in Antwerp today is from the diamond trade, a multibillion-dollar-a-year business shoehorned into a pair of streets near the central railway station. It was into the diamond quarter that the Irishmen took the remaining paintings. Cahill had a contact there:

a diamond dealer who had handled industrial diamonds stolen by Cahill from a General Electric synthetic-diamond plant in Dublin. The dealer advanced one million dollars to Mulvihill in exchange for a share of the larger proceeds anticipated from some later disposition. The diamond dealer took possession of the art, sending it for safekeeping to a bank in Luxembourg. Hogan and Ellis followed this trail in the only way they could—at a distance behind the criminals, picking up leads supplied by informants, sifting through them, conducting surveillance. When they understood what had happened, they realized that the exchange in Belgium confirmed the emergence of a new kind of art theft.

This transaction—the pictures accepted as collateral against some future deal—seems simple. But before the Antwerp trade, the structure of such a transaction had only been conjecture. The men who had made the assumptions were Dick Ellis and his boss, John Butler, a detective chief inspector in Specialist Operations at Scotland Yard.

When Butler in 1991 took over the intelligence and organized-crime unit known as SO-1 (Specialist Operations 1), the unit included the Art and Antiques squad. The Russborough file was one of the first he reviewed. He found that Scotland Yard had spent a lot of time on the case, including the Naughton affair. He discussed it with Ellis, then with his superior. Both agreed that a lot of resources had gone into a chase that had at that time already strung out over five years, with little result. But the pictures were particularly important, and Butler found himself leaning toward a new commitment. "I made a conscious decision," he said, "that if we were to get involved, we would only do so if we had a proper strategy."

Behind the deliberations lay Butler's idea that they might be dealing with a new kind of trade in stolen art. Until then, he says, Scotland Yard classified art thefts into three categories. The first were those committed by specialist thieves, the true "art thieves"—

criminals who steal pictures or objects worth, say, forty thousand dollars, that are simple to fence because they are easy to introduce back into the legitimate art trade. The second were robberies to order, in which someone had identified an opportunity both of theft and disposal, and contracted someone else to commit the robbery. Third came "Dr. No," the nominal collector with huge resources and few scruples. In Butler's thinking, Dr. No could be the popular conception of the secretive billionaire, prepared to deal with criminals to achieve his ends, or—and here Butler took an important step—the end collector might himself be criminal. It was this thought that led to the formulation of a fourth category of art theft.

Police knew that criminals had entered the art world as collectors. The task of money laundering is the conversion of illicit cash into legitimate assets, which can later be sold for clean cash. For example, Butler had heard that Pablo Escobar, the Colombian drug lord, had assembled a collection of French impressionist paintings. "It seemed to me," said Butler, "that such a collector wouldn't be overly bothered by where his art came from. He'd quite happily buy on the open market, but also elsewhere. If he could do it, why not others?"

Moreover, art would confer status on the criminal owner, as it did in the parallel world of legitimate collecting. "If I'm a criminal, I may not understand a painting, but if I've got it I'm a top-of-the-heap criminal. And even if I paid top dollar for it at Sotheby's, I might *tell* people I stole it."

As Butler saw it, though, this new art trade had already morphed into a specialist subset, following the understanding by criminals that an object valued for one reason could be used for another: to buy drugs. It did not matter that the stolen object would be valued at a fraction of its legitimate price, because the cost of getting it was zero. If a Vermeer was worth three hundred million, the rule-of-thumb criminal valuation of 7 percent yielded a handsome twenty-one-million-dollar black-market value. Furthermore, it need not be paid for in cash but in kind. Out of such reasoning came the discovery by police of the principal use for high-end stolen art today—as collateral in the drug trade. This was Butler's fourth category.

"The reason it was worth thinking all that through," said Butler, "is that it changed the way we ran our covert operations. We used to pretend we were buying back for insurance companies." With the more sophisticated criminals interested in collateralizing art, however, Butler felt more complex operations were called for. "Most crooks will tell you they could walk into a crowded room and pick an undercover policeman out at a glance. The truth is, many of them could. We used to spend hours and hours trying to make an operation look conceivable to a criminal. Instead, you have to come at it another way. You have to make it *inconceivable* to them that the guy standing in front of them is a cop."

To meet this test of inconceivability, Butler and Ellis thought their actor would have to be foreign. They sorted through the possibilities. These included bringing in an undercover policeman from another country's force. This plan ran into problems with the concept of entrapment: Some countries forbid officers to obtain arrests through trickery. In the end, they found in their own ranks the player they were looking for. He had already successfully posed as an American. What is more, he had fooled Irish criminals.

Imagine a chessboard. The pieces were arranged in a complex way. Cahill had white. He understood how all the players were supposed to move, so that was not a problem. His problem was that he had always stayed remote from the play and never met his opponent face-to-face. He would rely upon Mulvihill to make the actual moves. This was Cahill's weakness. If he had been at the board himself, with all his innate suspicion, he might have been able to see that one of the tall, white-looking pieces now to be put in play was not really white at all; it was the black queen in disguise. Butler and Ellis had put it there. The black queen was Charley Hill.

B Y AUGUST OF 1993, Hogan and Ellis knew the remaining Beit pictures were in Antwerp, and had begun to plot the endgame operation against Niall Mulvihill and the Belgian diamond dealer. Hill would play a shady American with, as he put it himself, "an interest in art opportunities." He took the name Chris Roberts.

By bringing in Hill, Butler and Ellis had involved another unit of Scotland Yard, SO-10, the undercover squad. In any covert operation, it was this unit's task to supply tactical necessities, not only the operatives themselves but the whole apparatus to support the sting: airline tickets, cars, hotel rooms, clothes to suit the identity of undercover agents. They would also perform the crucial liaison with foreign police. In the operation against the Irish gang the undercover unit was represented by its head, a detective sergeant identified by his alias, Sydney Walker.

In the usual way, through their moles inside the target gangs, Scotland Yard introduced Hill to the criminals. The sting played out over the expected obstacle course of feints and missed meetings, of suddenly changed plans, of the antics of criminals alert for traps. All this time Cahill was probing for a sign that the Garda had him in play. He did not find it because Hogan had the door shut tight; if indeed there had been a Garda leak, as Scotland Yard suspected, Hogan had sealed it. Cahill's final test, relayed by Mulvihill, was a demand that Hill go to Oslo, where he would be vetted by Cahill delegates sent there for the purpose.

Hill agreed and went. He took a risk in doing so, because there was a chance that one of the Irishmen would be Tommy Coyle

Limerick
County Library

(whom Hill did not know as a Garda informant). Hill, in the guise of Charley Berman, had of course met Coyle eight years before. The Berman identity had been blown when Tom Bishop, the FBI "mafioso" introduced to Cahill's gang by Hill-as-Berman, had dropped an FBI confidence slip on the table in front of Coyle and two other gang members. Hill and his handlers were gambling that this time Cahill would send someone other than Coyle, and he did.

"They liked me," Hill later recalled. "They'd all come up from London. They were Cahill's London guys, with Niall Mulvihill." Hill didn't know it at the time, but the Irish crooks thought he was gay. Scotland Yard's mole inside the gang had told them so. According to Hill, who found out later and beamed with pleasure at the recollection, the detail would have made him more believable. "It was brilliant. Criminals slag [malign] each other all the time. It made me seem like the genuine article, and they probably felt better thinking they knew something about me."

While the game advanced this way, with the players making their moves and countermoves, a shadow game was also afoot. In this other contest, the object was to understand the larger purpose of the play. Cahill was bending himself to the daily task of directing his chess pieces on the distant board, but not only that. He was also setting in motion an amazingly sophisticated scheme, so that, when he got the money he expected, he would have the means to deploy it wherever he wished. The police suspected this activity, and their part in the shadow game was to unravel it.

The first thread investigators tugged was Oslo. Hill's meeting there with the Irishmen had taken place under the auspices of a crooked Norwegian lawyer. Scotland Yard discovered the lawyer had been part of a plan to sell fraudulent securities into the Frankfurt market. When detectives focused on his connections, they found a Dublin criminal financier with ties to international money laundering. Inquiries about this newly discovered player went to

Interpol, and information on his activities came back. Police began to search for his place in the Cahill puzzle.

T HE CURTAIN went up on the final act on the morning of August 14, 1993, when Niall Mulvihill got into his red BMW and drove out through the gates of his home in Dublin's Ballsbridge. With Garda surveillance teams tailing him all the way, Mulvihill crossed the Liffey and drove north to the airport. He looked like any other businessman as he walked through the terminal in his dark suit, briefcase in hand, and boarded the 7:10 a.m. Aer Lingus flight to Brussels.

At the same time, three accomplices moved into place to support Mulvihill: An Irish national boarded a Brussels flight at London's Heathrow airport; another Irishman, already in Belgium, drove to the airport to meet his two compatriots; and a Yugoslav "heavy"—a bodyguard—drove to a bank in Luxembourg, picked up the Vermeer, and headed west back into Belgium to wait for the others in Antwerp. Hill and Sydney Walker flew into Brussels, rented a car, and took the expressway for the thirty-minute trip to Antwerp.

At 10:30 a.m. Hill and Walker entered the old city and drove along the Schelde. They turned up past the Old Town Hall and made their way through the busy streets and the tangle of streetcar lines and into the broad boulevard of De Keyserlei. The last block of the grand thoroughfare, before it ended at the extravagant, pink stone railway station, was lined with sidewalk cafés. They parked in front of the Alfa De Keyser hotel, a small establishment favored by the diamond trade, only a street away. The Alfa De Keyser's rooms were comfortably fitted with easy chairs and desks and the usual minibar, but were not customarily supplied, as a certain third-floor room had been that day, with hidden microphones and lenses and direct audio links to the Belgian federal police and Scotland Yard. The Yard in turn had an operator connected to Phoenix Park, where Liam Hogan waited at the phone. The streetscape of De Keyserlei was the usual bustle of strollers and tourists and café habitués. It would have been hard to notice, mixed in among this population, agents of the ESI—Escadron Speciale d'Intervention—the Belgian police unit charged with surveillance and the actual physical business of arrest. They had filtered into the avenue throughout the morning, so as not to alert the criminal countersurveillance they had spotted sitting with their espressos in the sun across from the hotel.

So everyone was in place with something to watch when Niall Mulvihill came along the sidewalk with a spring in his step and went into the hotel. He had one of the London Irishmen with him, and they went straight up to Hill's room. Walker's presence would be natural and expected; no important criminal would attempt to conduct such a transaction without the support of a bodyguard. In the room the visitors verified the price for the four pictures and were shown Hill's certified check for two million dollars. This completed Hill's part of the business: proving that he had the money to do the deal. The Irishmen now had to show that they had the goods. If both parties were satisfied, they would arrange a final meeting to exchange pictures for cash. Mulvihill handed Hill a key to the trunk of a car and told him where to find it. Walker would remain with Mulvihill while Hill went alone to verify the art.

The car was around the corner, in a parking garage on Langeherentalse Straat behind the diamond quarter. It was late morning when Hill walked past the barrier and up the ramp into the concrete structure. The building was gloomy but not dark. Daylight leaked in through horizontal slots, and the ranks of parking spaces were illuminated with fluorescent light. In the August heat the garage was heavy with the smell of cement and engine oil.

He found the car on the third level, a silver Saab with Belgian plates. "The big Yugoslav was standing there cracking his knuckles," Hill recalled, "and I just opened the trunk and there was the Vermeer." Hill paused as he recounted this part of the story, because the missing Vermeers—the Beit and the Gardner—were the holy grail of the world's art police at that moment. As he well appreciated, an object of almost incalculable value lay in the opened trunk. "There was no frame, no glass," he said, more charmed than awed by the memory, "and I picked it up and held it in my hands. I had no doubt it was the real thing. The only doubt I had was whether the Yugoslav might knock me on the head and dump me into the trunk. But by then they'd decided I was the real thing."

Thinking to protect himself against treachery by arranging that only one of the four pictures be brought from Luxembourg, Mulvihill had made a potential blunder by picking the most valuable painting. The purpose of bringing a single work was to make sure that the purchasers did not seize the whole parcel before payment of the money. But the picture he had brought, the Vermeer, was so valuable and important that snatching it, even at the risk of losing the others, would have seemed logical to any criminal. In fact it seemed logical to Hogan too, and presented him with a terrible dilemma.

Through his line to the operational command in London, Hogan had the Vermeer effectively in sight. It was Irish property, and so it was up to the Irish to decide whether to sweep aside the rest of the game and grab the Vermeer, or wait for Mulvihill to produce the other paintings. A national treasure lay in a trunk within easy grasp. Adding to this pressure was the personal one that it had been Hogan's father whose gardaí had recovered the Vermeer in 1974. If the painting slipped out of Liam Hogan's hands now, and he failed to get it back, he would lose what his father had won. "I knew if I put it to Conroy he'd say, 'Grab it,' so

I didn't. We showed them the money, made a date for them to come back with the whole load, and let them drive off with the Vermeer."

The ESI had meant to tail them, but the Belgian watchers spotted a countersurveillance around Mulvihill. Fearing that the criminals would detect the police, Hogan gave the order to cut the tail. The Vermeer vanished down the road.

Mulvihill returned to Dublin. The second Irishman went back to London and the third to Brussels. Police shadowed them all. Luxembourg "minders" had the Yugoslav in sight.

Hogan waited in agony. The date for the next meeting, August 28, came and went. Mulvihill stayed put in Dublin. Hogan hardly left the office, and even when he went home he could not sleep. "The truth is, we weren't even a hundred percent sure where the paintings were. I thought Luxembourg, but at that time we didn't know."

Early on September 1, Mulvihill alerted Hill that they were ready to trade. The exchange was set for the next day in Antwerp. Ellis passed the news to Hogan.

Less than an hour later Mulvihill drove out of his gate and crossed the river, heading for Dublin airport. He was followed all the way. By the time he got to the airport, a young garda in plain clothes had already bought a ticket for the Brussels flight and was waiting in the departure lounge. Mulvihill came in, looked briskly around, and paced back and forth beside the seats until the flight was called. As before, the Belgian police were in place for his arrival and had a tail on him from the moment he came through immigration.

One of Mulvihill's Irish accomplices had arrived from London and was waiting for him outside the terminal. He led the way to the parking lot. The two men got into a rental vehicle and headed out of the airport and onto the expressway north for Antwerp. An unmarked Belgian police car drifted into the traffic behind them, keeping well back. They were not afraid of losing the Irishmen, having the advantage of already knowing their quarry was headed to Antwerp.

In Dublin, Liam Hogan had arrived at the Phoenix Park and was sitting in his tiny room listening to a minute-by-minute report on the unfolding operation. The person feeding him the bulletins was Jill McTeague, a Scotland Yard detective manning the communications desk in London. The British had operational control, since their people, Walker and Hill, were the units on the ground. McTeague sat linked to a chain of policemen relaying reports from the field, and that chain had been extended to Hogan.

This period of time, as the sting came down to its crucial moments, was the hardest for Hogan. He was remote from the action, when his every instinct as a policeman was to be in the thick of it. But more important, the investigation of Cahill's international connections was producing, piece by piece, clues that pointed to an astonishing and wholly unsuspected ability to shuffle funds. By the time Cahill's deputies were exiting the motorway and threading their way through Antwerp to sell the most valuable thing he had to sell, Cahill had prepared a place to receive the money: a bank in the Caribbean island of Antigua. It was not simply that he had opened an account; he had bought the bank.

Not long before noon, McTeague passed the news to Hogan that the Yugoslav, having visited the bank in Luxembourg, had crossed into Belgium and was nearing Antwerp. The excruciating question was: What did he have in the car? At the previous meeting he had brought only the Vermeer. Would he have all the pictures this time, or perhaps a parcel that did not include the Vermeer? It still preyed on Hogan's mind that the Vermeer had been within reach only two weeks before, and he had let it go. If he failed to secure it now, the responsibility would be his alone.

He did not have long to wait.

Promptly at noon three cars drove into the Antwerp airport

parking lot: Mulvihill and one of the Irishmen in one, the Brussels-based Irishman and the Yugoslav each in separate cars. Hill had been waiting for them, and he and Mulvihill went into the terminal. Hill handed the Dubliner a briefcase full of cash. At his post in Ireland, Liam Hogan was experiencing the last pangs of doubt as he waited to find out what the criminals had brought. Hill and Mulvihill went outside and opened the trunk of one of the cars. Inside were Metsu's *Man Writing a Letter*, Vestier's *Portrait of the Princesse de Lamballe*, and a few charming fakes of Picasso and Degas, thrown in for free. There was a golf bag in there too, and rolled up inside, the Goya. And lying there on its own, collecting dust, was the Vermeer. Hill gave the signal, and the Belgians came screaming into the parking lot in a pair of BMW sedans, four agents in each.

"They were wearing their *Miami Vice* T-shirts and cotton sports jackets and were all tooled up with their Dirty Harry specials," Hill later recalled. He was still technically under cover, so they grabbed him, too, and spread him on the ground and pushed his face against the pavement.

When McTeague gave him the news, Hogan made the short walk to Noel Conroy's office and gave him the tidings. The story passed quickly into the hands of the Garda press office and swept onto the front pages of the Irish papers. For the detectives, though, the work was far from done.

I N THE ENSUING MONTHS, Hogan and his colleagues at Scotland Yard uncovered an eye-popping maze of criminal exchanges through which Cahill had meant to launder money and acquire drugs. The art had already moved along some of these routes: from Dublin to Northern Ireland to London to Istanbul, and from Dublin to London to Antwerp to Luxembourg and back to Antwerp. Drug shipments were to flow from Istanbul to Dublin, and from Marbella, Spain, to Antwerp to London to Dublin. These illegal routes were child's play compared to the labyrinthine path the money was to follow. It would move from Dublin to Antigua to London. From London, some money would return to Dublin, while other funds would skip over to the Isle of Man, be deposited there, and then return to London to be dispatched to Oslo for transfer to Frankfurt.

Cahill did not mastermind this; he had people who could. The crooked Dublin financial adviser had the contacts necessary to take control of the Antigua bank. All Cahill had to do was provide the money. It was true that his old gang was mostly in jail, and the attentions of the Tango squad had squeezed him hard. But Cahill needed little real money to set this extravagant serpent of a scheme in motion. He had the Vermeer.

The Antwerp sting and the disentangling of the complex circuitry for the exchange of art for drugs proved beyond doubt the

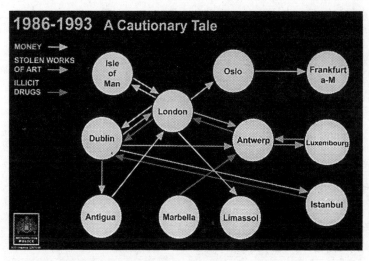

Diagram showing the routes of money, drugs, and stolen art.
(Courtesy of Dick Ellis, from a diagram prepared by him for Scotland Yard)

145   *Liam's Game*

rightness of John Butler's and Dick Ellis's formulation of a new "fourth category" for stolen art: collateral for drugs. Certainly, some thieves steal paintings and sell them for cash; but the headline-grabbing, multimillion-dollar thefts seem destined to end with the pictures circulating endlessly in the underworld as a kind of scrip, valued at some fraction of their worth. "It's a very good commodity for criminals," said Detective Sergeant Vernon Rapley, in 2003 the head of Scotland Yard's Art and Antiques squad. "If they steal a major painting, we do them the great favor of publicizing it and showing its image in the newspapers, together with its value, which means they can go to their fellow criminals and use it as collateral, as a down payment on drugs and firearms. The provenance is provided by the newspaper report that says this painting is worth so many millions of dollars."

The Irish Vermeer had passed into this desolate realm when the diamond dealer advanced one million dollars to Cahill's representatives, taking the picture as surety. As the deal was later understood, Cahill was to buy drugs with the advance, to be shipped from Marbella, and repay the dealer with interest. The Vermeer could then be used again in a like arrangement. The Antwerp sting caught the Vermeer just at the point where it might have slipped for good into this shabby role, lost to the public forever.

{ 9 }

In Vermeer

THE FOUR PICTURES rescued from the Yugoslav's trunk had been out of the public view for seven years and did not return to it directly. They receded into the custody of the Belgian police. The police told reporters that the Beit paintings would be secured in the central precinct in Antwerp; this was a deception. Believing that the Irish criminals had a link to the IRA, the Belgians feared a raid by well-armed guerrillas intent on recovering the loot. Late on the night after the sting, and in the strictest security, a little convoy of police vehicles pulled away from the station on Quinten Matsijslei. They drove three-quarters of a mile in the direction of the River Schelde and pulled up at a small, black door at the rear of a huge neoclassical structure—the Koninlijk Museum voor Schone Kunsten, Antwerp's art museum. With advanced security and a staff trained to protect art, and helped by the false lead that the pictures were with the police, the museum seemed a safer hiding place.

The Irish pictures went into anonymous, locked print-drawers. The only outsider to visit them was Andrew O'Connor, who traveled to Antwerp on September 8 to view the paintings and verify that they were indeed the missing Irish property. That night O'Connor stopped in Brussels to meet the Irish ambassador, Patrick Cradock, and discuss the repatriation of the pictures.

Cradock had just taken up his appointment, and the two men dined alone in his newly painted dining room, with unpacked crates lined along the walls. They talked about the paintings far into the night, and Cradock outlined the steps they would have to take to get them. An energetic man, and much taken by the project, the ambassador had already spoken to the Belgian foreign ministry, who had confirmed that the art was "available for return to the National Gallery of Ireland." However, before the investigating magistrate in Brussels would release the paintings, he required two documents: a formal request from the National Gallery, and a formal assertion detailing which of the pictures stolen from the Beits now belonged to the gallery.

Like the mills of God, the machinery of Belgian justice ground its deliberate way through the matter of the Irish pictures. One month gave way to another, as papers shuttled to and fro between Dublin and Brussels and the magistrate concluded his investigations. Finally, the last *i* had been dotted and the last *t* crossed, and on April 26, 1994, Andrew O'Connor arrived in Antwerp to take the paintings home.

Waiting for O'Connor in the basement print room were a pair of Dutchmen, Ben Broos, chief curator of the Mauritshuis museum in The Hague, and Jørgen Wadum, the museum's chief conservator. They had come down to look at the Vermeer. Broos and Arthur Wheelock, Jr., the leading American scholar of Vermeer, were planning the greatest Vermeer show ever, a joint project of the Mauritshuis and the National Gallery of Art in Washington, D.C. The show was to open in Washington the next year, 1995, and the organizers wanted to inspect the condition of the Irish Vermeer and see if they could get it for the show. They had asked O'Connor if they could come and look at it.

What followed that morning in Antwerp was the second important discovery about the Vermeer, a discovery as fascinating and unlooked-for as O'Connor's own revelation about the sealing wax twenty years before. It created, almost by accident, a new school of thought about how Vermeer produced an effect that viewers find so beguiling: the arresting perspective accuracy of his compositions.

J ØRGEN WADUM had been a soldier in the Royal Lifeguards in his native Copenhagen. Among his normal duties had been stints mounting patrol in his blue dress uniform in front of the Amalienborg palace, and he was part of the saluting guard at the funeral of King Frederick IX. Wadum displays a wonderfully definite and meticulous nature, and it is easy to imagine him as he then

Jørgen Wadum, chief conservator at the Royal Cabinet of Paintings Mauritshuis
(Conservation Department of the Mauritshuis, The Hague, 2003)

In Vermeer

was—a spruce, young figure in a spotless tunic. When his military service was done, he enrolled in Copenhagen University's conservation program, and in January 1990, he took up his position at the Mauritshuis.

The Mauritshuis owned two Vermeers. One was *View of Delft*, Vermeer's only landscape, a painting that so moved Marcel Proust when he saw it in The Hague in 1920 that he wrote: "After seeing [it], I realized I had seen the most beautiful painting in the world." In 1993, Wadum was at work on the museum's other Vermeer *The Girl with the Pearl Earring*. The *Girl* was in terrible shape. Her varnish had yellowed with age. The picture had been restored in the past, and the old retouches had discolored so much that they looked like shadows: Her blue headband was splotched with them. Age cracks cobwebbed her forehead and cheeks. Such cracks, called *craquelure*, are the natural product of time, as the paint dries and gets brittle and the surface opens into fissures. Some of this craquelure had been made worse by previous restorers, who applied a further "painted craquelure."

When paint cracks with age, the crack curls up at the edge, where the surface layer pulls away from the painted "ground." This creates tiny, concave chips, what Wadum called *cupping*. The surface of the *Girl* was a sea of cups, and sometime in the past a restorer had tried to flatten them. To soften the paint, the restorer had attacked it with aggressive solvents. The assault had succeeded, in that the curled-up edges eased back down. But the solvents deformed the sharp edges of the paint along the cracks, making them look as if they had been melted, as in a sense they had.

So the edges of the cracks looked blurred. This created an aesthetic problem. The viewer's eye is used to cracks in old paintings. Although they mar the surface, they reinforce a sense of venerability. (Forgers understand this and diligently add craquelure to forgeries of old paintings.) But the edges of the cracks should be sharp, and the restorer had made them soft. To correct this unpleasing effect, and narrow the cracks that he had widened, the restorer painted in dark edges. This attempt to match the widened, blurry cracks with the original cracks is what is meant by painted craquelure.

The disfiguration was particularly bad on the left side of the *Girl's* face and on her forehead. Even the cracks that had not been deliberately darkened were clotted with old varnish and discolored wax. Elsewhere, whole patches of paint had fallen off, a victim to hostile climate and storage conditions in the past and to being bundled about Holland from owner to owner at a time when the painting was merely a domestic chattel, worth considerably less than the fake pearl dangling from its subject's ear. Despite the havoc of time, Wadum thought that the basic integrity of the structure was intact, and well able to withstand the face-lift planned for it.

The restoration swept the veil of time from the maiden's face and let the light of day onto her fresh skin and lustrous eyes. Her earring glowed. When the work of restoration was complete, the "Dutch Mona Lisa" gazed out afresh, returned by craft and diligence to a condition closer to the one her maker gave her. "More than any other Vermeer," a critic had written of the painting a century earlier, "one could say that it looks as if it were blended from the dust of crushed pearls."

The Mauritshuis occupies the former town residence of a royal prince. It stands on the edge of the Hofvijver, or "palace lake," in the old center of The Hague. Wadum's studio was in a basement room built out under the lake. A skylight, set just above the surface of the water, admitted an aqueous light into the restorer's room. In this grayish radiance, Wadum was plunged into the closest study of Vermeer's craft—a technical study by a technician. The finest details of how the paint related to the canvas absorbed him. Vermeer was "aware of the effects of a colored ground on the overall tone of the paintings," Wadum wrote in *Vermeer Illuminated*, his record of the restoration of the *Girl*. "The hue of the ground, warm or cold, is important particularly if it is overpainted with thin, transparent layers of paint. For the *View of Delft* Vermeer used a warm, brown-gray color. For *The Girl with the Pearl Earring* he used a cool gray ground."

Minute paint chips removed by scalpel from the edges of the canvas revealed beneath a microscope the composition of the paint: a cake of brilliant, blazing fragments of ultramarine, of grains of sand that glowed like amber. Wadum's knowledge of the physical structure of Vermeer's work grew swiftly; but not only his physical knowledge. Something like tenderness crept into his notes. "The transitions on the cheeks and around the nose, from pink to greenish shadows, are soft and smooth. The brushstrokes cannot be seen with the naked eye. Clearly, specific painting techniques were deliberately used to obtain a smooth, flowing effect."

As Wadum's understanding expanded, so did his speculations. "Purely by accident," he said, he began to wonder how Vermeer had achieved his magical perspectives. He rejected the solution offered by the camera obscura theory, a theory then popular, that the painter had used a kind of camera to project an image of the subject onto the canvas and had then traced the image. Wadum's intimacy with Vermeer's craft, with the painter's absorption, layer by painstaking layer, in the construction of an image, would not admit the possibility that this paragon had *traced* a picture. It seemed deceitful—a trick not worthy of Vermeer. "I didn't like it. Also, we don't find a lot of books in the catalogues of Vermeer's possessions, so how did he know about it, and how it worked? It doesn't make sense. I hate it."

The Netherlands is a rich dominion for the contemplation of perspective in seventeenth-century painting. Interiors came off the easels of Holland in regiments. Wadum raked through them for a clue to Vermeer's technique. In the catalog of a 1991 Rotterdam show of Dutch church interiors, he came across a reference to pinpricks that had been discovered at the vanishing points of several pictures. In perspective painting, parallel lines converge at a notional place called the vanishing point—the point at which they seem to meet. If you stand in the middle of a long road, you will see the same effect: In the distance, the edges of the road appear to meet. Interior painters produced this effect by making parallel lines—the lines between tiles, say, or the aisles of a church—converge in the painterly distance. The effect convinces the eye of distance and right perspective. The reference to pinpricks suggested that the painters had used compasses to help them in the composition, although exactly how they had used them remained a mystery. Then Wadum found a pinprick himself, in a painting by Frans Franken the Younger made between 1615 and 1617. Obviously, at least to Wadum, the punctures in the canvas had a direct connection to technique: The painters had stuck something into the canvas and used it to help create the illusion of space.

In the summer of 1993, with this problem whirling in his head, the conservator took his family to France for the summer holiday. Unable to leave his obsession behind at the Mauritshuis, he took some catalogs along. They showed the works of artists such as Pieter de Hooch and Gerard Houckgeest, whose interiors draw the eye confidently into the depths of the pictorial space. Nothing is amiss in these interiors. The lines run straight back into the far reaches of the image. The painters who made these pictures were contemporaries of Vermeer.

In his rented house in Burgundy, Wadum continued to puzzle over the problem. He went into a store in the local village and bought sheets of plastic. In the daytime, he and his wife would range through the surrounding country, taking long walks and enjoying the summer weather. In the evening Wadum would clear the dishes from the dining table and spread out his catalogs. He traced the pictures onto plastic and set the point of the compass at the vanishing point. The windows were thrown open to the warm night, and Wadum lost himself in the experiments: cutting the plastic, piercing it here and there with the point of his instrument, searching for a relationship he was certain existed. At the end of the holiday he had still not found it. He returned to The Hague in September, just in time to read about the Belgian police swooping into the airport parking lot in Antwerp and rescuing the Irish Vermeer.

S EVEN MONTHS ELAPSED before Wadum could see the picture. He had no idea that his search for a solution to the problem of perspective was about to end. He wanted to look at the Vermeer, as did Ben Broos, solely to judge its fitness for inclusion in the coming show. Finally, on April 22, 1994, O'Connor faxed: "I will be in Antwerp at Hotel Industrie Monday next 25 April. The picture will be packed on Wednesday at 1400 so please ring me so we can meet and examine the picture together. I look forward to seeing you again."

Wadum and Broos arrived in Antwerp the morning of the twenty-sixth. The museum's director, Lydia Schoonbaert, met them at the back door. "It was amazing," Wadum later recalled, "like being in a film. It was very hush-hush, because the Belgian police didn't want anyone to know where the paintings were." The visitors presented their passports for inspection, clipped white-plastic identification tags to their lapels, and followed the director through a steel door into a large, low-ceilinged basement room.

The print room of the Antwerp museum was an antiseptic space: white floor, white walls, white ceiling, everything illuminated by harsh fluorescent light. Low, white-metal cabinets of wide, thin drawers lined the walls. An attendant slid open one of the drawers to reveal the Vermeer, "just lying there," said Wadum, "as if it was some print."

The party crowded around, anxious to see if the painting had suffered in its long sojourn in the underworld. To their relief, it had fared well. They examined it and tipped it this way and that, marveling at how it had withstood its long captivity. All agreed the Irish Vermeer was in excellent shape. O'Connor had cleaned and revarnished it only twenty years before. In terms of seventeenth-century paint, it sparkled. Wadum admired the restoration. He stepped back from the table and cocked his head, and that is when something fresh jumped out at him.

The picture lay flat on the table in a raking light. The light source was quite powerful and the topography of the painting sharply revealed. Wadum and Broos were chatting as the conservator studied the picture, but Wadum's words trailed away. He stopped listening. In a moment he had his head loupe on and had stepped to the table and bent over the Vermeer. He had noticed a straight line, cutting through the relief. He picked the picture up in his hands and peered at it. Deeply incised lines ran along the edges of the floor tiles. Wadum had never seen such lines in a Vermeer. He did not think they existed in any other picture.

"We were looking at it and I took it up in my hands," Wadum later remembered. "It was a very late painting, and Vermeer was continuing to experiment, and I was looking for ways he might have changed his technique and that drew me to the writing woman's left eye. In the center of the eye a pinprick pierced the canvas. I said, 'Andrew, there's a paint loss here.'"

Wadum pointed out the indentation to O'Connor. O'Connor said he knew it was there. He'd seen it when he had restored the painting. He had put it down to age—some little injury sustained in the long life of an object that had shuttled from Holland to Vienna to Paris to London, and finally to a damp palace in the Irish countryside. But Wadum felt the hole was not an accident. Its placement was too deliberate—dead in the center of the eye. Without really thinking, "almost on a whim," he fished in his bag and found a piece of string and held it, one end to the eye and the other end on one of the lines of perspective. When he did this, it was as if the tumblers of a safe clicked in his mind and the door swung open. Wadum saw, with perfect conviction, the answer to the question that had been racking him: how Vermeer had created, in such small spaces, perspectives so convincing that the eye follows them in utter confidence around the painting, and in the case of *Lady Writing a Letter with Her Maid*, clear out the window and into the chalky light.

Wadum's theory is devastatingly simple. The pinprick could mean only one thing: that Vermeer had pierced the canvas with a pin to which a length of string was fastened. The pinprick became the vanishing point, and from it Vermeer could pivot the taut string out to any sector of the canvas and establish a perspective line along it. As Wadum showed, such lines do in fact meet at the vanishing point of the pinprick.

In Wadum's view, Vermeer would have applied chalk to the string and snapped the string lightly against the canvas, transferring the line of perspective directly to the surface, where he could trace it. The conservator pointed out that this method— the transfer of chalk from a taut string—was used by contemporaries of Vermeer as well, and even today, by painters of trompe l'oeil interiors.

"For me that made Vermeer also a craftsman, who knew the shortcuts to work in a very straightforward way. I believe the artists of the seventeenth century used whatever means they could find to proceed as quickly as possible to the image they wanted. The painter is the one who transforms what's around us into art. They were trying to make the perfect illusion of a room. I was excited by it, because being a conservator, and looking at paintings through a microscope, it was thrilling to me to see that these theories of camera obscura were not right."

A CAMERA OBSCURA is an optical device with an ancient pedigree. Basically a pinhole in the wall of a darkened chamber, the camera appeared in Europe in the thirteenth century as a means of observing eclipses of the sun. Light entered the darkened room through the pinhole and projected an image of the solar event onto the opposite wall, where, in the words of a writer of the day, "it is possible to see the crescent-shape getting smaller as the moon covers the sun."

The first idea that such a viewing system might have implications for art seems to have occurred to Leonardo da Vinci, who in 1490 wrote that if the image of outside objects admitted into a darkened room through a tiny hole is projected onto a piece of white paper, "you will see all the objects on the paper in their proper forms and colors. . . . These images, being transmitted from a place illuminated by the sun, will seem as if actually painted on this paper."

It is a long way from this observation to the theory that Vermeer used a camera obscura to compose his paintings, and the man who made the journey, Philip Steadman, did not knowingly set out on it. Steadman is an architect and the professor of built form studies at the Bartlett School of Architecture, University College, London. He began his long investigation of Vermeer in the 1980s, while living in the village of Olney, in Buckinghamshire. He was then a lecturer in design at the Open University, an institution for correspondents. One of the courses Steadman gave was architectural drawing for engineering students. How to represent an architectural volume on the two dimensions of a sheet of paper—that was the challenge. Practical exercises harnessed the technique of drawing to the need

In Vermeer

to depict three-dimensional space. In the course of such exercises Steadman taught the mathematics of perspective geometry, which enables the calculation of the angles of perspective in any representation from the known size of depicted objects. Dutch interior paintings of the seventeenth century abound with scenes knotted together into the most convincing perspectives. Happily, there were objects of a known size in some of the pictures. Vermeer's rooms, for example, contain Delft tiles, and the size of these tiles has remained the same from Vermeer's day to our own.

For the math in the student exercises to work out, certain assumptions had to be made about the pictures. For example, if a rectangle were depicted, one had to assume, to get a proper mathematical result, that each corner contained an angle of ninety degrees. Steadman knew they did not. In a seventeenth-century house erected on the sodden plain of the lower Rhine, no straight line would have held true for long.

Nevertheless, Vermeer's perspectives *looked* perfect. The interiors—there are eleven—exhibited that snapshot realism. They seemed correct. Like Wadum, Steadman found himself wondering how the painter had achieved the feat. The pictures came to absorb him. As a way into the problem, he asked himself whether each of Vermeer's interiors showed the same room.

They seemed to. Light raked in from a window on the left. An elaborate, distinctive mullion pattern in the glass was repeated in some of the paintings. The skirting tiles at the base of the walls and the floor tiles were the same from picture to picture. Some of the furnishings changed, but not all. However, the scale varied. *Lady Writing a Letter with Her Maid*, for example, is about eight inches higher and six inches wider than *A Lady Standing at the Virginal*. To compare the pictures, Steadman decided to make them all the same size.

From the known dimensions of a skirting tile, he forced copies of all eleven pictures into a uniform scale in relation to the tile.

Applying perspective geometry to the same-scale reproductions, he concluded that they were indeed the same room. Still, he felt he needed more evidence, and on a trip to Delft he visited the Raadhuis, the seventeenth-century town hall. The attraction was the furniture. The staterooms are furnished from the seventeenth century. Steadman hoped to find some object that matched the appearance of one of Vermeer's props. If he found it and could establish that its dimensions were the same as one of Vermeer's, he would have gained another scale marker. He already had the skirting tiles; one more known size would give him extra geometric insurance. Armed with photographs, he went through the Raadhuis room by room. Nothing matched Vermeer's furniture.

Returning to Olney, Steadman tackled the challenge again. He selected a tapestry chair that appeared in three pictures: *The Concert*, *Lady Seated at a Virginal*, and *Girl with a Wineglass*. Adopting the assumption that the rooms were all the same room, and that he had correctly analyzed the various angles of perspective, he calculated, from the known size of the skirting tiles, the dimensions of this chair.

Dutch archival records showed that the chair had been one of a consignment of forty-one, and Steadman wondered if one might have survived. He took a photograph of the chair from a Vermeer catalog and sent it, with his calculation of its size, to Marc van Leusen, a Delft architect, asking him to see if he could find one and measure it. Van Leusen showed the photo to a keeper at the Prinsenhof museum, who remembered seeing a chair just like it in the attic. Up they went, and there in a cluttered room beneath the roof, tumbled in among boxes and contemporary chairs and covered in a fine, thin layer of Holland dust, was a chair exactly like the one in the paintings. Van Leusen measured it. Steadman's figures were correct to within a centimeter.

Shortly after, van Leusen found a much more famous Vermeer object—the chair with the lion's-head finials—seen in *The Music*

Lesson, Woman in Blue Reading a Letter, Young Woman with a Water Pitcher, A Lady Writing, and *The Girl with the Red Hat.* Van Leusen measured that chair, too, and again found Steadman's projected dimensions to be very close.

By the late 1980s, Steadman's research was absorbing much of his waking time. "You could say I was starting to get into the grips of an obsession," he admitted. At the heart of this obsession was the question: How had Vermeer managed these exquisitely faithful paintings, in which he had captured the geometry of his subject down to the minutest calculation of angle? Such unusual fidelity seemed to suggest photography, a sensation familiar to many admirers of Vermeer. In 1861 a pair of French scholars, the Goncourt brothers, described Vermeer as "the only master who has made a living daguerreotype of the red brick houses of that country." Daguerreotypes were early photographs.

Others have observed such photographic details as the largeness of the officer's hat, and indeed the officer himself, in *Officer and Laughing Girl,* compared to the girl. The officer is sitting in the foreground, and in a snapshot the viewer would expect him to be larger than the girl, who occupies the middle ground. But Vermeer's contemporaries would have been inclined to render them closer in size—what Steadman calls the "psychological" perception rather than the strictly proper depiction of perspective. Finally, he could not resist the conclusion to which he had been moving step by step over the years: Vermeer's pictures looked photographic because the painter had used photography.

In Steadman's view, Vermeer had constructed a camera obscura at one end of his room by erecting a partition and installing a lens. He would then have sat in the darkened cubicle and traced the image projected onto the back wall. Steadman amassed many facts in support of this. He calculated, for example, that if a lens were placed at exactly that point where the perspective of any given picture showed the point of view to be—in other words, where the painter would have been sitting to see the room as he had painted it—the image projected onto the rear wall of the enclosure would have *exactly the same dimensions as the painting*. Steadman believed that Vermeer himself had revealed his technique, and that a tiny patch of black in a mirrored sphere suspended from the ceiling in the *Allegory of Faith* is the booth of the camera obscura: the painter's coy admission of his method.

In 1987, confident in his assumptions, Steadman built a one-sixth scale model of Vermeer's room as depicted in *The Music Lesson*. His house in the village of Olney had once belonged to a printer, and there was a large, bright room where the press had stood; this is the room that housed the model. Steadman took enormous pains, not only replicating the geometry but purchasing tiny wooden figures from an art-supplies shop, dressing them in period costumes, and styling their hair as Vermeer had pictured it. He made a little virginal, and put it in, and added chairs, a table, a rug for covering the table, a mirror. (Steadman's five-year-old daughter was so ravished by the model that she begged to play with it.) At one end of the model he placed a camera, so that the lens occupied the pictorial point of view as Steadman had calculated it. The picture he obtained was a near-perfect, scale replica of the painting.

Two years later, in 1989, the British Broadcasting Corporation decided to build a full-scale reproduction of Steadman's model of the room, to test his theory. The BBC hammered the room together in the Bristol television studios. They dressed the finished set to match *The Music Lesson* and costumed the actors exactly as painted by Vermeer. To interview Steadman, they rigged him out in seventeenth-century Dutch dress and draped him in a massive, reddish wig. He said his daughter thought he looked very nice; more satisfactorily for Steadman, the full-scale experiment duplicated the results he had obtained on a smaller scale after almost ten years of grinding away at the math and scouring Delft for furniture. Steadman's theory, that Vermeer was in effect a copyist, is contested by, among others, Arthur Wheelock; but the theory expanded into a kind of preeminence on the helium of its impressive evidence, until Wadum showed up with his notional pin.

O N THE EVENING OF April 26, Liam Hogan arrived in Antwerp to escort the paintings home. They were packed the next day by Gerlach, a firm of Dutch art shippers. The following morning at nine o'clock, the truckers loaded the art into an unmarked vehicle. Gerlach preferred to ship through Amsterdam, and so when the work was done and the truck secured, they pulled away from the Antwerp art museum and set off for the Dutch border, with Dr. Schoonbaert, as O'Connor remembered, "visibly relieved to see the pictures leave."

O'Connor and Hogan followed the truck in a Gerlach car, and Belgian police provided escort. At the border the convoy halted. The Belgians said good-bye, and two Dutch police motorcycle escorts took up position and sped the Irish treasures straight to Amsterdam's Schiphol airport. As in all such transfers, security was a paramount concern, and the arrangements for moving the pictures had been kept secret.

So far so good: The paintings were slipped anonymously through the busy airport and onto the plane. As valuable art, they would not ride in the cargo hold. The paintings were carried onto the plane before the boarding call and installed in their own seats at the back. Hogan and O'Connor sat in the row in front of them. At last the passengers boarded. Just after two o'clock in the afternoon, the Aer Lingus flight lifted off from Schiphol and turned west across the North Sea. "We were just starting to relax," O'Connor said, "when the pilot came onto the public address and welcomed everybody aboard and then right out of the blue announced: 'I'm sure you'll all be happy to know we're bringing our Vermeer back home!' Liam and I just stared at each other."

T HE GOYA was the most severely damaged of the paintings. It had been roughly rolled, and paint was flaking off in several places. The canvas had been sliced from its frame with a razor or sharp knife, and there were slice marks on the surface where the blade had slipped. In Antwerp, O'Connor had performed first aid by applying strips of tissue paper impregnated with wax to the worst of the injuries, to hold the damaged surface in place for the return to Dublin. The fate of the Goya had a special poignancy. In a note on the Beit collection written while the pictures were still in Cahill's hands, Sir Alfred had confessed that the missing portrait affected him for personal reasons. "The sitter, Doña Antonia Zárate, is far from being a sentimental woman (indeed quite the reverse) but it was under this picture that I successfully proposed to my wife, and lived happily ever after."

When O'Connor turned his hand to the Vermeer, he felt a particular satisfaction. The thick, waxy, matte finish he had applied twenty years before had protected the surface well. There was a slight abrasion and some paint loss on the maid's dress, and a tiny indentation in the lower left of the painting. O'Connor stripped off the varnish, repaired the damage, and revarnished the picture in a clear finish. When he was done, the Vermeer was set in a new frame made for it by the London master framer Tim Newbery. The frame was a gift of Sotheby's, the auctioneers, whose chairman, Lord Gowrie, had often been at Russborough as a boy with his parents, as guests of the Beits. He said that he had first learned to love pictures at Russborough, wandering the rooms of the old palace by

In Vermeer

himself and gazing at the Beits' collection. The frame was an homage to that boyhood pleasure.

When the Vermeer was hung for the first time in its new home, the National Gallery held a reception to welcome it. The staff kept the guest list short and did not publicize the event, for fear of raking up fresh stories about the theft. Lord Gowrie flew in from Dublin, and Lady Beit came down from Russborough. When they had finished admiring the smart, new frame and complimented O'Connor, and drifted off through the rooms, two Irishmen, a father and a son, remained in front of the Vermeer. They gazed at it for a few minutes in silence, until one of them spoke.

"If they lose it again, they can get it back themselves," said Liam Hogan to his father.

Ned Hogan pondered this remark and then amended it. "If we get it back again," he said, "we keep it."

The Scream

EFFECTS RIPPLE OUTWARD from the tossed stone of a crime. The thefts of the Irish Vermeer led to discoveries which, while they might have happened anyway, equally might not. Similarly with the crime's solution—it set up a momentum. The Irish sting had assembled a package of talents at a single time and place: Scotland Yard, 1993. In the shifting priorities of policing, this unit would not stay together long. But it was intact four months later and ready to be used again when another picture, more famous than the Vermeer, fell into the hands of thieves, and a straight line of impetus may be drawn from one sting to the next.

The crime in question happened on a snowy February morning in Oslo, Norway. That day—Saturday, February 12, 1994—the Olympic games were to open in Lillehammer, two hundred miles north of the Norwegian capital. A horde of press and officials had come streaming through Oslo on their way, and the city had rung with the sound of reveling. But now the bars were empty and the streets deserted. A gray dawn was showing in the sky. The thin light had just begun to seep into the streets and to illuminate the fairy-tale-yellow royal palace on the hill above the town.

Ladder at the broken window of the National Gallery of Norway.
(Scanpix Norge-Forlagsavdelingen)

I suppose that at that hour a footman was making his way up to the king's bedroom with the morning coffee. King Harald had a long day ahead: He and the queen were going up to Lillehammer to open the games. It was to be a special pleasure. The king's father, a much-loved sovereign, had been a passionate skier; *skikonge*, the Norwegians called him——the skier king. There is a bronze statue of this monarch, striding along on his skis on a hill above Oslo. Yet not everyone was swept up in this happy congruence, for while the king and queen were rising to prepare for the journey up to Lillehammer, three of their subjects, a pistol shot downhill from the palace, stole a ladder from a building site, put it in their car, and headed for the National Gallery of Norway with felonious intent.

At half past six they turned into Universitetsgata and parked on the street in front of the brown brick building. While one man waited in the car, the others took out the ladder, put it against the main façade, climbed up in no particular hurry, broke a window on the second floor, and clambered through. A closed-circuit camera captured everything. They turned left when they got inside, walked twelve yards, and unhooked a single picture from its place on the front wall. They penciled a note—"thanks for the rotten security"— and pinned it to the wall where the picture had hung. Then they went out the window, climbed back down, left the ladder where it was, and drove off into the February dawn.

When employees at the National Gallery arrived later that morning to find a ladder leaning by the front door, and quickly discovered the theft, they telephoned the Oslo police headquarters. And so it was that at nine o'clock that morning Leif A. Lier, the most famous policeman in Norway, on a day when he had looked forward to watching on television the opening of the Olympics, instead walked from his house to a waiting police car and was whisked across the city to the scene of the crime.

Lier is a striking figure—tall and heavyset, with silver hair and a florid complexion. Reporters followed him around the country from crime to crime, filling their pages with accounts of criminals that Lier brought low. From his office on the fourth floor of the police headquarters building in the Grønland district, he looked south over the harbor and far down the fjord, where it glittered away for miles between green slopes until it was lost from sight. From that vantage point it feels as if the whole of Norway lies there beyond the window, as indeed it does. Lier's job sent him everywhere in the kingdom, as long as the crime was horrible enough.

Leif A. Lier
(Courtesy Jørn-Kristian
Jørgensen, Oslo police)

One of his early successes—it was front-page news for weeks— was cracking a grisly crime in the village of Ørstra in the northwest of the country, seven hundred miles from Oslo. Two brothers named Antonsen, a pair of dullards, were suspects in the kidnap, rape, and murder of a twelve-year-old girl. The investigation was flopping around uselessly until Lier went up and put one brother in a cell in Åndalsnes and the other in Bergen jail, two hundred miles away, and broke them in a week.

In another headline crime, Israeli intelligence agents assassinated a Moroccan living in Norway, mistaking the man for a Black September terrorist. The Norwegians caught five Israelis within three hours— two at the Oslo airport and the others in a raid on an apartment. Israeli intelligence has a fearsome reputation, and in the ensuing investigation Lier moved his wife and children out of Oslo to his brother-in-law's house in Drammen, forty miles away. He slept with a loaded pistol by his bed. This was probably not the life envisioned for him by his parents, active in a different kind of force: the Salvation Army.

By 1994 Lier had risen into the highest ranks of the national police. He was a household name in Norway; his autobiography, *Travels in Murder*, became a national best-seller. An ordinary theft would not normally have dragged Leif A. Lier away from the Olympics on that February morning, but this was no ordinary theft. The picture the thieves had taken was *The Scream*, Edvard Munch's masterpiece of twentieth-century anguish. *The Scream* is easily one of the best-known images in the world and certainly the most famous object in Norway.

So Lier rode through the city to the gallery. The ladder still leaned against the wall. A blue-and-white police tape cordoned off the scene. Lier went upstairs to have a look at the blank space where *The Scream* had hung. He read the note, removed it, collected the security tape from the closed-circuit camera, and left. "We watched the whole thing later," he recalled. "It took them two minutes. We couldn't identify anyone from the tape, because it was terrible quality." He smiled, then shrugged. "Our main concern was always, first, get the picture back."

Lier fed the message out to his criminal contacts that if anyone wanted to put a favor in the bank, this would be the time to do it. Nothing came of this. He had a suspect, a gangster named Pål Enger. Enger had stolen a Munch painting before—*The Vampire*, taken from Oslo's Munch museum in 1988. That time he'd been caught. Lier thought the criminal might have decided to give Munch another try and had seized upon the opportunity of the winter games for cover, when police resources would be taxed by extra security demands. Still, Lier could find no useful leads.

The investigation shuffled fruitlessly along until, one month after the robbery, a story in an Oslo tabloid caught Lier's eye. It was a profile of the Art and Antiques squad at Scotland Yard, fresh from its sting on the Irish gang. As it happened, another case was taking Lier to London, so he called John Butler and arranged to meet. On a blustery March morning Lier took a taxi from his hotel to a triangular, gray stone-and-glass building on Broadway in central London, a short walk from Westminster Abbey.

JOHN BUTLER and Sydney Walker were waiting for Lier in Butler's large, fifteenth-floor office. The sweep of windows gave a regal view of Buckingham Palace and St. James's Park. As head of SO-1, Butler was at the top of his game. He was a man who dreamed in Technicolor, an impresario of the sting, and at this moment in policing history he had at his disposal a movie mogul's range of props. His unit kept a yacht docked at Southampton to support operations that called for the illusion of a rich conspirator. One of Butler's schemes had called for chartering a Boeing 747 jumbo jet. He wanted to convince his targets—major drug dealers based in the Caribbean—that his operative was an important hood, and screaming in to an airstrip meeting in a private behemoth seemed a good way to make the point. In every case the aim was to present a charade so convincing that criminals would not think to question it, and he had already worked out such a scheme for Lier.

Butler and Walker had not been surprised when Lier had called; they had expected it. From the moment Butler had read about the theft of *The Scream*, he had decided that Scotland Yard would help recover it if asked. This decision reflected his thinking that all art crime was international crime, and that at some point in the efforts to dispose of a picture like *The Scream*, London would figure. So he had met with Walker and Dick Ellis, and the three had quickly sketched out the broad shape of a sting. They had decided that the most credible buyer of such a famous picture would be someone posing as the representative of an institution with deep pockets— one the criminals would accept as easily able to ransom the picture.

The scene in Butler's office on that morning was surely one of the oddest in the annals of policing. The crime was a mere month in the past. It had happened six hundred miles away in the Norwegian capital. At Scotland Yard none of the investigators knew the suspected thieves, nor the country, nor any of the complex lore that distinguishes one criminal milieu from another. All they really had were two advantages: an unmatched comprehension of how crooks move art, and the sheer, exhilarating confidence that they could sting the Norwegian blackguards and deliver them to Lier. They had the whole thing figured out and could have handed it to Lier in an envelope. But it is not the nature of policemen to be open with their thoughts; they told Lier they would mull the matter over and get back to him.

When Lier left, Butler waited until late in the afternoon and then called Dick Ellis, who was in California on a personal mission. Ellis came from a long-established family in Cornwall, a defiantly chauvinistic county that sticks out into the Atlantic on the south-western tip of England. Cornishmen will tell you they are not really English at all, and one of their sports, ocean rowing in fiendishly cumbersome boats, is a means of flaunting their uniqueness. In California Ellis was reconnoitering the coast in preparation for a row. A crew of twenty-one similarly minded sportsmen had proposed to row, for charity, two whalers down the entire length of the Golden State from the Oregon border to San Diego, a distance of five hundred miles. By *whaler*, a Cornishman does not mean the fiberglass runabout popular with American cottagers, but an altogether more sullen, bullheaded craft of lapstrake construction, twenty-seven feet long, which seven sturdy men need all their strength to bludgeon through the sea.

Accompanying Ellis were some rowers from the FBI. He also knew people in the Los Angeles police and, from other investigations, at Los Angeles's J. Paul Getty Museum. When Butler called him about Lier's visit, then, Ellis was ready to execute their agreed plan: to introduce an undercover policeman from the Yard into the negotiations for *The Scream*. The agent would pose as a representative of the Getty, acting purely out of altruism to restore a national treasure to the Norwegian public. Ellis went directly to the Getty with this proposition, and its officials readily agreed to go along.

Not surprisingly, Ellis, Butler, and Walker had one person in mind for the role: Charley Hill. Not only had Hill performed brilliantly in the Irish sting, but he had turned in another winning performance in Ellis's recovery of Pieter Brueghel the Elder's *Christ and the Woman Taken in Adultery*, in which he had posed as a benefactor of the arts.

Ellis gave the museum the personal details of Chris Roberts, Hill's alias for the Norway operation. Although he had used this alias in Antwerp, Scotland Yard doubted the Norwegians would know about it. One night a senior official of the Getty slipped the fictitious particulars into the Getty's employment list. They issued a payroll number, calling cards, and a Getty ID. They backdated a letter of appointment. If anyone had been able to get far enough into the Getty's staff records to check out Chris Roberts, they'd have found he was a bona fide employee, attached to the director's office.

WHEN LIER RETURNED to the Norwegian capital from London, his task was to make contact with the thieves. They proved wary. Several attempts to lure them out failed. The police fed false leads to informants, who spread them around Oslo. Lier was not discouraged when the bait went unnibbled by the fish. He believed the picture was still in Norway. He thought that the thieves, like Cahill, had hit the gallery because it was an easy target. They had a plan for stealing the painting but no plan for its disposal. Getting rid of it would now be their preoccupation. If the thieves were too suspicious to fall in with an opportunity supplied by the police, the police would have to wait for an opportunity to be supplied by the thieves. They did not have long to wait.

There was an art dealer named Einar-Tore Ulving who lived in the district of Vestfold, in the city of Tønsberg, some sixty miles south of Oslo. Tønsberg sits on the western shore of the Oslo Fjord, within easy reach of the capital, and from a pleasant suburb Ulving ran his international business, specializing in Munch. He prospered. He had a helicopter and two Mercedes-Benz cars. He enjoyed a wide repute, and late one afternoon an anonymous caller rang him up and offered him *The Scream*. Ulving promptly called the police, as presumably his contact had expected, for no sooner had the caller finished talking to Ulving than he, the caller, dialed up the National Gallery of Norway and asked for the chairman of the board, Jens-Kristian Thune.

The caller's story was that he had not himself stolen the picture, and didn't know where it was, but, for a price, could put Thune in touch with the people who had it. The chairman heard him out, then called Lier. Thune told Lier that his caller wanted to meet face-to-face. Lier understood that the calls to Ulving and Thune were to demonstrate that the stolen item was in play. He told Thune to go ahead and meet the caller.

The call to Thune came on a Thursday in late April. The next evening he drove east out of Oslo to the village of Lørenskog, fifteen miles distant, in the hills. There was no surveillance on him. Lier thought the caller would have countersurveillance on the scene, and decided against a tail. The policeman's only precaution had been to advise Thune to meet his contact in surroundings where there were other people. Thune picked a restaurant in a mall.

On Saturday morning Thune came to police headquarters, looked at some mug shots, and picked out his interlocutor. The man, he reported, wanted to broker the return of the picture to the gallery, with Einar-Tore Ulving, the art dealer, as middleman. Lier told him to signal his agreement, and the chairman left. Lier called John Butler to tell him *The Scream* was in play.

In every sting, the first operational challenge is to persuade the target to swallow the identity of the deceiver. In the Irish game, Scotland Yard's Irish criminal mole had vouched for Hill. Scotland Yard and Lier naturally began looking for a way to introduce Hill into the orbit of the Norwegian crooks who had contacted Thune. They had not yet found a way, when they caught a lucky break. Billy Harward, an Englishman who had served time in a Norwegian prison, sent a message to Lier that he knew how to recover *The Scream* and would sell the information for fifty thousand pounds. Lier agreed to go to London for a meeting and notified Scotland Yard. Ellis arranged Lier's accommodation at the Grosvenor House, a hostelry on Park Lane.

Lier was on his guard, for Harward had been so embittered by his prison term in Norway that he'd sworn, upon leaving the country, that someday he would kill a Norwegian policeman. Instead, he came into Lier's room at the Grosvenor in high spirits and immediately picked up the phone and ordered drinks. Hill, in the guise of Chris Roberts, was also present, as a guarantor that money was available to ransom the picture back, an arrangement no government could have made. (Governments do not pay ransom, and in some jurisdictions it is an offense for anyone to make such payments to thieves. That is why the exchange is always structured as a payment for information.)

An atmosphere of bonhomie arose, fed by the drinks and the opulence of the room. The mood was further helped by the five thousand pounds handed over to Harward by Lier—a down payment on the full fifty-thousand-pound fee. Harward was in such a good mood when he left that he hugged the big Norwegian.

No useful information came from Harward, and the rest of the money was not paid. Yet the contact accomplished what for Ellis was its mission: feeding Hill's "Chris Roberts" identity into the criminal ambit. It is not known whether Harward passed the information to Norwegian connections, but he might have. Such a tip would have further bolstered Hill's credibility when, finally, his name and Getty identity were passed to Thune, who gave the information to Ulving. Ulving, acting for police, fed the name to the criminals. Hill had been successfully slipped in. In the parlance of Scotland Yard, the sting for *The Scream* "went live."

A BUZZ OF ANTICIPATION developed. Phones began to ring in Oslo and Tønsberg with questions about the picture, and how it might be delivered, and who would pay for it, and when and where. In London, Ellis, Butler, and Walker were briefed by Lier. Walker's undercover unit, SO-10, would actually be running Hill. In the plan they had worked out, Walker would accompany Hill as his "assistant." The Norwegians who had the painting would immediately recognize Walker as a bodyguard. This would make Hill more believable, because they would not expect him to arrive with a large amount of cash and no protection. A man with no protection in such a situation is either an idiot or a cop.

At Scotland Yard, the detailed plan for the sting was signed off and ready. On Wednesday, May 4, Dick Ellis went to the cash room and handed in his chit for half a million pounds. The cashiers had the money ready, a mix of large and small notes, and Ellis counted it carefully. Then they packed the bills into a suitcase—"a good-sized grip," said Ellis—and he took it to his office and locked it there for the night. "I was a little nervous," he admitted. At five o'clock the next morning he handed the money to Butler, who would travel to Oslo himself to run the sting on the ground. Hill and Walker left for the airport, and that Thursday afternoon, with Walker accompanying him, Hill came into Oslo on the British Airways flight from London, larger than life, turned out in Gap khakis and a blazer, a perfect vision of American vraisemblance.

Hill and Walker went straight to the Grand Hotel, a gray stone dowager in the center of Oslo, across the street from the Norwegian parliament. Butler flew in separately and took a taxi to the SAS Plaza Hotel near the central train station and checked in. At the Grand, Hill and Walker took a suite at the front, with a view onto the boulevard that runs up to the royal palace. Hill called Einar-Tore Ulving in Tønsberg, and an hour later an arsonist and thief named Jan Olsen called Hill back. Olsen said that he, in company with Ulving, would meet Hill and Walker that night, Thursday, at the Plaza.

According to Ulving, a gentleman whose life was about to sail into a choppy sea, the meeting was to have been a simple introduction, where the players, among whom he did not number himself, would eyeball each other and make whatever arrangements such people make. Ulving's role, as he saw it, was that of a facilitator. He was connected by family to Jens-Kristian Thune, the National Gallery chairman, and had undertaken the meeting at Thune's behest. Once the introductions had been effected, Ulving thought, he himself would return to Tønsberg. But this was not to be.

Olsen announced that Ulving must remain at the hotel, or the deal was off. Right then and there, he booked a room for Ulving, and Ulving, not seeing an alternative, took it. Feeling somewhat adrift, Ulving telephoned Thune several times that night. Thune asked him to see things through. Soon, Ulving lost even this contact, when Thune suffered a heart attack at his seaside home and was rushed by helicopter ambulance to a hospital in Oslo. Ulving went uneasily to bed.

In the morning a second surprise awaited him when he came down to the lobby to meet Hill and Olsen for breakfast. They found themselves in the midst of a police convention, gathering there at the hotel. Officers from forces across Scandinavia were milling around in the reception areas and restaurants. The convention had nothing to do with Lier's arrangements, but was there by happenstance. Moreover, it was Butler who had booked the Plaza, from London, and he had no idea the convention had been planned. By Ulving's account, Olsen was a man of considerable aplomb. He surveyed the scene with a wry expression. Perhaps he accepted that no one stalking him would devise a trap that included filling a hotel with masses of visible police, some in uniform. So the four sat down and had their breakfast. Walker explained that his own task was to vet any proposed arrangements, to protect "Chris Roberts" and the money, and to ensure that neither went astray. Olsen heard him out, then said that he had to leave to consult his fellows, and they all agreed to meet again that afternoon, when Olsen would inspect the show money. Under the circumstances, Olsen would have preferred another locale, but Walker said that the money was in safekeeping at the Plaza, and that is where it would stay for now. Olsen left.

When Olsen returned, he and Walker began to discuss the minutiae of the transaction—how the money would be exchanged for the picture without either party betraying the other. Ulving says that Olsen had a good head for details and seemed determined to evolve a scheme in which every action, down to the smallest move, must be clearly defined and understood. His English was not good, and Ulving had to repeat in Norwegian whatever Walker said. (Unknown to Olsen—and, for that matter, Ulving—Walker, married to a Norwegian, understood everything Olsen said.)

All the while, as the discussion went back and forth, Olsen had been scrutinizing the room. Ulving says that Olsen obviously began to notice, mixed in with the conventioneers, men who seemed not to be part of the program. These were Lier's surveillance officers, and, said Ulving, "Olsen spotted them one by one. Finally he said, 'You know, this place is full of cops watching us.'"

"No," said Hill when this was translated, "I don't think so."

"Just look over at the bar," said Olsen. "That guy with the newspaper has been sitting with a beer for an hour and he hasn't touched it." Without warning Olsen sprang up and marched to the bar, snatched the man's newspaper from his hand, and dug a thumb into his belly. "How come you are sitting here with a bulletproof vest!?" Olsen shouted at the man.

As Ulving recalled, the man mumbled something about being on a training exercise and rushed out. Hill and Walker seemed crestfallen by the incident, but Olsen said, "Let's go ahead with the money show."

The money was in a safe-deposit box in an office behind the reception desk, and Walker led Olsen to see it. Hill and Ulving remained in the lobby. As Ulving remembers, Olsen's demeanor changed once he had viewed the money. "You could see the greed and excitement when he came back. He really wanted that money now that he had set eyes on it."

Suddenly Olsen insisted they all drive to Oslo airport, where Hill and Walker were to rent a car. Apparently Olsen wanted to confuse police tails by adding another vehicle to those they would have to follow. At the airport, Olsen told Hill and Walker to meet him back at the Plaza, and drove away with Ulving. Ulving was at the wheel. When they got into the outskirts, Olsen began to issue a series of instructions: turn here, then there, along this street, stop, go back. At last Ulving found himself on a darkened street with a wall on one side. "Turn in here," said Olsen.

"There's nothing to go into," Ulving replied.

"Just turn," snapped Olsen. As they did, a concealed door opened in the wall, and Ulving drove into a garage. The door rolled shut behind them.

The Scream   178

For an hour, Olsen's accomplices swept the car for bugs and electronic tracking devices, even claiming to find one in the apparent hope of tricking Ulving into an admission that one existed. It didn't, and when the criminals were satisfied, Ulving and Olsen got back in the car and headed off on a tour of Oslo back streets, the container port, and the tunnels that pierce the city's mountains— all the while Olsen checking for a tail. He found none.

Around midnight, Olsen, Ulving, Hill, and Walker met again in front of the Plaza. "Olsen told us, 'It's now or never,'" Ulving recalls. "He said the time was now to do the deal, or they would destroy the picture, and the next thing we would see would be a piece of it, and after that, another piece. We were talking about this, and Charley Hill was sitting there in the backseat of my car, with the door open, and one foot in and one foot out."

Ulving believes that Butler, from his hotel room in the Plaza, at this point ordered his officers to suspend the operation for the night. The Scotland Yard detectives returned to the Grand, and Olsen gave Ulving new instructions: He was to drive, by himself, southward on the E18, the main highway to Tønsberg. He was to keep to this road, and would receive new instructions by cell phone.

Ulving left the city. There was little traffic, and he drove the Mercedes station wagon fast. Within half an hour he was whisking along the expressway across the inky waters of the Drammenfjord. The main road south traverses forests and farms. The lights of villages twinkled in the distance. In places a view opened to the Oslo Fjord—at that time of night, more a black waste than a visible expanse of sea. Ulving was alone with his thoughts, and they were dark. "The police didn't have a clue where I was; that's what I realized. They were not following me. I was completely on my own."

His cell phone stayed silent all the way to Tønsberg, and since he had received no instructions, Ulving headed for his home. At

The Scream

one o'clock on Saturday morning, he pulled into the driveway of his mansion. No sooner had he entered the front door than the phone rang in the hall. He picked it up and a man's voice told him to get back in his car and drive north again, up the E18 in the direction of Oslo. He would receive instructions on the way. "I felt a little chill," Ulving recalled. "Obviously they had followed me from Oslo, and knew the moment I set foot inside my house."

He had driven for fifteen minutes back up the Oslo highway when the cell phone buzzed and a rough voice directed him to pull into the parking lot of a roadside café. There was no other car in the lot, and the restaurant, closed for the night, was dark. He waited for a few minutes, until a man with a balaclava covering the top of his face appeared from behind the café, walked to the car, and looked in at Ulving. The man, a criminal named Bjørn Grytdahl, was carrying what seemed to be a painting, wrapped in a blanket. He got in the car beside Ulving and ordered the dealer to drive them back to his house to await instructions.

Ulving refused. "My wife and two children were at home. I think this man had a gun. There was something making a bulge in his jacket. He insisted that we go to my house, and I refused again. I would not do it."

Ulving suggested that they go instead to his summerhouse in Asgårdstrand, a village not more than half an hour by road from Tønsberg. Asgårdstrand is an artists' summer colony, its tidy houses stacked like fresh laundry on the steep shore of the Oslo Fjord. Ulving's large, wooden summerhouse sits by the water outside the village. At one-thirty he and Grytdahl pulled in behind the house. In May the summer homes were still shut up, and no lights shone anywhere in the vicinity. The house itself was cold and bare, the pictures all in winter storage. Grytdahl made Ulving take him through the entire house, examining every room and opening every closet

Einar-Tore Ulving with his wife and children in front of their summerhouse at Asgårdstrand. (Courtesy of Einar-Tore Ulving)

until the criminal was satisfied they were alone. Then, by a single lamplight, he unveiled the painting.

"I had no doubt at all. It was *The Scream.* I knew this painting very well. In fact, I had a valuable lithograph of it in the car at that very moment, between sheets of cardboard, and I was afraid he might discover it, and take that, too. I took a good look at the surface of the painting, and then the back. So then he wrapped it again in the blanket and put it in the basement. He turned out the light and we sat in the living room in the dark. He hardly spoke more than a word. I knew I had lost contact with the rest of the world, that no one knew where we were. There was no sound but the wind, and the fjord lapping on the rock. It was most unpleasant. I just sat there and smoked."

At about five o'clock, Ulving decided he had to act. Within a few hours, he thought, Olsen would reestablish contact with Hill and Walker, and he did not want to spend the intervening time waiting in the lonely house by the fjord. He suggested to Grytdahl that they change cars. Ulving had another Mercedes—a powerful 500 SLR sports car. He thought that driving such a car might appeal to Grytdahl, and it did. "He liked the idea, so he agreed. We left the painting in the basement and drove to my house in Tønsberg."

Ulving disliked returning to his home with Grytdahl, but felt he had to. He went inside and told his wife that everything was all right. Outside, Grytdahl eagerly took the keys and got into the driver's seat, and he and Ulving pulled away. For the next hour they sped around the smaller highways in the vicinity of Tønsberg, while Grytdahl enjoyed himself at the wheel. For Ulving, the most pressing matter was to make a connection with the outside world. He knew his wife would have alerted the police, but he had no idea how things were proceeding. With Grytdahl's assent, he called his cousin, Gro Hillestad Thune, Jens-Kristian Thune's wife, and said he needed instructions. She checked with Lier, who said that Ulving should play the game out as it unfolded.

Ulving then called Olsen, who was back in touch with Hill. Ulving suggested that they all meet—Ulving, Grytdahl, Hill, Walker, and Olsen—at a roadside restaurant at Drammen, southwest of Oslo on the highway to Tønsberg. Olsen agreed, and later that morning the five men met at the wayside establishment. Just then, a bus pulled in, and the passengers began streaming out and heading for the restaurant. Ulving thought that in the confusion he might escape, but Olsen grabbed him and shoved him roughly into the car.

In Ulving's recollection, Olsen was fired up to get the deal done. The sight of the show money was still fresh in the criminal's mind. His concern was to make sure that he got his hands on the money as soon as the painting was revealed, and since the painting was now in Asgårdstrand, that was where he meant to go. Walker, however, suggested that Olsen's plot contained a flaw: Everyone would be together in Asgårdstrand while the money was in Oslo.

He proposed that Hill and Ulving go to Asgårdstrand alone, while Olsen and Grytdahl accompany him back to Oslo. Hill would call Walker once he had the painting safely in hand, and Walker would release the money to the two Norwegians. Strangely, Olsen agreed, and as he and Grytdahl climbed into a car with Walker, and Hill and Ulving headed south alone, the criminals' three-month run as possessors of one of the world's best-known paintings came to an end. Instead of *The Scream*, they had a veteran, undercover cop. If the sting had been made of steel, this would be the moment when its teeth were snapping shut.

The crooks had a half-hour drive back to Oslo. Ulving and Hill were about forty-five minutes from *The Scream*. They found it wrapped in its blanket in the basement. Worried that the gang might have accomplices around the house, they wedged the painting into the narrow space behind the seats of Ulving's car and drove to a nearby hotel, making sure they were not followed. Ulving owned the hotel, which had not yet opened for the season. They forced the back door and hurried inside with *The Scream*. Hill called Butler, and Butler called Lier. By then, Olsen, Grytdahl, and Walker had arrived back at the Grand, and from his office in Grønland, Lier ordered: "Arrest them."

Undercover police do not automatically break cover when their brother officers move in for an arrest; a cover identity may survive the springing of the trap. So when Lier's officers burst into the suite at the Grand and handcuffed Walker, he shouted, "Run!" The police caught Grytdahl, but Olsen got away.

"Strangely," Lier remembered, "he went home."

Olsen had an apartment in the suburb of Stovner, six miles north of central Oslo. When he got there, he telephoned Lier and, in a rather senseless gambit to distance himself from the crime, said he knew where to find *The Scream* and would give Lier full particulars in exchange for a break. Lier told him to come into the

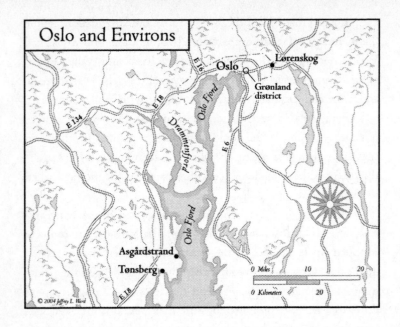

Oslo and Environs

police station and they could talk about it. Olsen replied that he had just spent all his money and could not afford a taxi. Lier told him to call one, and the police would pay for it when he got there. They did, and locked him up.

They grabbed suspected mastermind Pål Enger and arrested Ulving too. The dealer was quickly released, and the others were charged. They were convicted and later appealed on the grounds that the British undercover policemen had entered Norway under false identities—hence, unlawfully. They won.

Six years later, Pål Enger laid hands on a Munch again, this time legally, when he bought an unsigned lithograph by the artist at an Oslo auction. "A fabulous day," crowed Enger to the press. "To win the bid for a genuine Munch was just wonderful."

The Norwegian sting was the last great operation for the team that had come together at Scotland Yard. *The Scream* had been returned to the National Gallery of Norway, and *Lady Writing a Letter with Her Maid* was safely back in Ireland. Facing a declining budget, John Butler left the yard. Charley Hill succeeded him, a move that shifted a master actor from the stage to the producer's suite. Perhaps it was inevitable. "The problem was," Dick Ellis said, "Charley was dying of overexposure." Then Hill left the unit too, first to join an insurance company and later to start his own business as a private art detective. He became the media-friendly gumshoe in a number of high-profile cases, including the recovery of the marquess of Bath's Titian and the retrieval of a pair of Turners for London's Tate Gallery.

Dick Ellis walked straight out of the Norwegian sting into a famous art-world scam known as the Egyptian antiquities case. Ellis broke it, busting a ring that was buying Egyptian treasures, disguising them as modern fakes, shipping them into London, and restoring them. In 1999 Ellis, too, left the Yard.

In Dublin, Liam Hogan made inspector. Noel Conroy became commissioner. Tommy Coyle, the fence, died of cancer at the age of fifty, after a long career playing a double game.

In Oslo they rehung *The Scream*—a long way from the windows.

{ 11 }

The Irish Game

I N IRELAND, in the aftermath of the Antwerp sting, Martin
Cahill's reputation as a master criminal lay in ashes. He hatched
a number of schemes that reveal a man desperate to recoup his fortunes. He planned to steal the Book of Kells, the ninth-century
illuminated manuscript that may have been the only object in Ireland worth more than the Vermeer. Another plot was to snatch the
Sam Maguire Cup—the All-Ireland football trophy of the Gaelic
Athletic Association, to Irish sportsmen a totem worth more than
the Vermeer and the Book of Kells combined. Clearly, the once-
powerful General was straining for a single stroke that would
restore his lost preeminence.

Cahill's fate was sealed by his own indomitable pride and by a
turn that history took three months after the raid in the Antwerp airport parking lot. On December 15, 1993, the British and Irish prime
ministers issued the famous Downing Street Declaration, which
granted standing to Sinn Féin, the political arm of republican forces,
in talks on the future of Northern Ireland. Protestant loyalists in the
north, viewing Sinn Féin as nothing but a front for the IRA, were
enraged by the announcement. They vowed to carry a campaign of
terror south into the republic. Five months later they struck.

On the night of May 21, 1994, a Saturday, Sinn Féin had taken over the Widow Scallans pub in Dublin for a fund-raising event. More than three hundred people were jammed into the second-floor party room when, just before eleven o'clock, a car turned the corner into Pearse Street and pulled up in front of the pub. Two men got out, one carrying an overnight bag. They entered the pub and took the stairs to the upper floor. Guarding the door at the top was Martin Doherty, a thirty-five-year-old IRA man. He must have been suspicious from the moment he saw the two appear, because they were strangers and, even more alarming, one had a bag. Doherty tried to block them; they shot him four times, killing him instantly. A second man, inside the room, was felled by gunshots through the door and died. Failing to force the door, the men shoved the bag against it and fled, dashing outside into the waiting car and making their escape. Police swarmed to the scene and seized the bag. They found an eighteen-pound bomb inside. Somehow, the device had failed. If it had detonated, hundreds of IRA supporters would have suffered death or injury. The IRA saw the attack as the gravest of insults. Within days the UVF, a pro-British militia, took responsibility, promising to follow up with more attacks on the IRA and Irish civilians in the south.

A belief took hold in the IRA that Dublin criminals, in some ways the IRA's natural competitors, had conspired with the UVF, providing them with intelligence about the event and help getting in and out of Dublin. Because of his previous connection with the Portadown UVF, Cahill was summoned to a meeting by the IRA. He refused to go, telling them his affairs were none of their business. In the circumstances it was an act of astonishing bravado, and in Martin Cahill's long chronicle of such acts, the last.

In the following months the IRA put one of their men in touch with Cahill, ostensibly to explore joint criminal activities, but really to get close to him. Cahill was ailing then, from diabetes. Sources paint the picture of a man in declining vigor. Maybe poor health had dampened his suspicious nature. He had heard the rumor, which was all over Dublin, that the IRA had marked him for assassination, and yet is said to have accepted the report of his new associate that the rumor was untrue. Cahill behaved like a man who had run his last race and was done with running. His movements became predictable. He slept with Tina Lawless at her house in Swan Grove and rose in the afternoon to drive to Cowper Downs and spend the rest of the day with Frances. This routine made it easy for the assassin, and on the afternoon of Thursday, August 19, a motorcycle slipped in behind the General as he made his daily journey. At three-thirty, at a stop sign on Oxford Road, the killer came up beside Cahill and shot him dead with a pistol at point-blank range.

Martin Cahill went to his rest in a cortege of ten black limousines, the nearest thing to a mafia funeral that Dublin had ever seen. He was buried beneath a ruined abbey in Mount Jerome cemetery. An enormous floral wreath bore the legend "*Que sera sera*, whatever will be will be." At the graveside, Frances Cahill stood with her arm around her sister Tina, stroking her hair. Each of them dropped a single red rose onto the coffin while a soloist sang, "Every time you touch me I become a hero." Three of Cahill's brothers were missing from the press of mourners; they were in prison. Most of his men were in prison. There was no Cahill gang.

In County Wicklow, the old palace south of Blessington stood as it had for 250 years, almost as much a part of that green valley as the trees. Lichen grew on the stones of Russborough. The beech trees that the first earl planted were ancient now. Clouds came spilling in from the Irish Sea, and from the top of the mountains a climber could look down and watch as the clouds sailed over and cast the valley into shadow; when the clouds passed, the sunlight returned to the hill and the long palace of Russborough House answered with a silver glow.

Sir Alfred had passed away in a nursing home in May of 1994. Lady Beit remained at Russborough alone. When the pictures came back, she hung them where she and her husband had hung them before. The Vermeer made its passage through Washington and The Hague, spreading the fame of Russborough. People came out to the house in the summer and trooped through the great rooms. In winter Lady Beit shut the house, reopening in the spring.

THE CONTEST BETWEEN Irish criminals and police takes place in a tradition of brigandage that stretches back through the whole of Irish history. The most famous Old Irish poem, sometimes called Ireland's *Iliad*, is *The Cattle Raid of Cooley*. It dates from the eighth century, with roots reaching back to the second, and describes a royal raid on a neighboring royal house. Clearly, the business of Irish kings was to rob other kings. The Vikings, too, made the island their raiding-cupboard. When the Normans arrived, they brought pillage of their own. The long and violent struggle against English rule continued the practice. Viewed against this pageant of misfeasance, the Russborough robberies look less like crimes and more like the natural passage of the years.

The wheel came around again on June 26, 2001. At about 12:40 p.m. a blue Mitsubishi Pajero 4×4 (stolen two days earlier in Dublin and bearing false Kildare license plates) and a white Volkswagen Golf GTI (stolen, false plates) turned off the N81, drove up the lane to Russborough, and went through the gates. They had timed their arrival to coincide with the end of a tour of the house, and, as they had expected, they met some traffic coming out as they went in. This meant the house would now be almost empty. There would be few witnesses. The two vehicles drove past the turnoff for the parking lot and proceeded into the forecourt. There were three men—two in the Mitsubishi and one in the Volkswagen.

Two of them pulled on balaclavas. Then the Mitsubishi bounced up the front steps and burst the door from its hinges.

Russborough House is very large, and not even Lady Beit, waiting for lunch in the private wing, heard the jeep drive through her door. When visitors are in the house, the main alarm is not active, because anyone wandering through a room would set it off. So the house was silent when the two thieves in balaclavas broke in. They seemed to know what they wanted, because they rushed straight through the front hall, through the dining room and tapestry room. They did not stop until they got to the music room, where the Gainsborough and the Bellotto hung side by side. They ripped them from the wall at 12:42 p.m., the time recorded by the alarm connected to the pictures. That alarm began to ring.

It rang at Blessington, and it rang at the divisional headquarters at Naas, and it rang inside Chief Superintendent Feely's head. The robbers hurried back the way they had come and out through the shattered front door. Their accomplice had sloshed some gas onto the Mitsubishi and set it alight. They all piled into the Golf and in a spray of yellow gravel went fishtailing out of the forecourt. They shot through the gates, skidded into the lane, and when they got to the N81 turned left for Blessington. Two minutes flat.

That the robbers turned left, toward the closest Garda detachment, suggests that they knew the Garda patrol cars were elsewhere at that moment. One was at Ballymore Eustace and the other on the road that runs down from the Wicklow Mountains into the village of Hollywood. Both these locations lie to the south of Russborough; Blessington is north. As the Golf shot up the highway to the town, the thieves tossed out fistfuls of spiky, metal shapes made of welded nails, to blow out the tires of any gardaí who might come after them.

They sped through Blessington and turned east, onto the road that leads to Blessington Lake. They ditched the Golf at the side of the road and set it aflame. Their intention was to steal the first car

*Mitsubishi abandoned in front of Russborough during
the 2001 robbery* (Irish Times)

that came along, and they sure tried. When Brendan Brown, a local
farmer, appeared in his car (Feely said it was an Opal; the *Irish
Times*, a Mitsubishi), one of the crooks hauled out a pistol and
waved him over. When he stopped, they dragged him from the car
onto the side of the road. As they did, the farmer snatched his keys
from the ignition and held them in his fist. The robbers shouted at
him to hand them over; he refused. They punched him and kicked
him and fired a pistol near his head. Brown would not surrender
the keys. "He was just the type of person," explained Feely, "that
guns and people don't bother him. He said, 'You're not taking my
car,' and that was that."

Unable to overcome their mulish countryman, the thieves
hitched the pictures under their arms and ran off up the road. At
about this time witnesses spotted a silver Nissan Almeida tearing
out of the parking lot at the nearby Russellstown picnic ground,

though no one could say if the robbers were in it. Whether they drove, hitchhiked, crawled, or ran the whole way back to Dublin, they successfully evaded the police. Back at Russborough, when an *Irish Times* reporter pointed out that the intruders had seemed to know exactly what they wanted, ignoring copies and seizing originals, a rueful Feely replied, "As far as I'm concerned, I wish they were *all* copies."

The crime sounds prankish—busting into an old, rich English-woman's Irish palazzo and stealing the Gainsborough again—but it had a dark side. The robbers hit Russborough on the fifth anniversary of the drive-by execution by criminals of an *Irish Independent* journalist, Veronica Guerin, as she sat in her car at a stoplight in Dublin. Guerin was in the midst of investigating a Dublin gangster. The false plates on the Mitsubishi had the same registration number as those of the murdered reporter's car. The message cannot have been other than a black taunt at the Garda. If one of the criminals' aims had been to borrow some of Cahill's glory, a second was to display that most characteristic Cahill trait: contempt for the police.

This time detectives were able to track down their quarry faster than they had in 1986. Fifteen months after the theft they raided a house on the south side of Dublin and found both paintings. The next day they held a press conference to announce the recovery, and the Belotto and the Gainsborough were delivered into the hands of the National Gallery. At Phoenix Park the gardaí could relax and congratulate themselves that this time they had got things sorted out with something like dispatch. This air of satisfaction lasted exactly two days.

Before dawn on September 29, 2002, a pair of Dubliners went riding out of town in another 4 × 4. They drove through Blessington, turned in at that familiar road, passed through the gates and up the drive and across the gravel forecourt and, at six o'clock in the morning, put the front bumper squarely through a ground-floor window of Russborough House. They took five pictures, including two by Rubens, one of which had been stolen twice before. Again—two minutes flat.

"What can you do?" said Russborough's administrator, posing the question on everybody's mind. "You go on having more and more sophisticated alarms, but they don't seem to deter them."

The robbery made page four of the *Irish Times*.

O N AN AUGUST AFTERNOON in 2003 I boarded the one o'clock ferry at Holyhead, on the Welsh coast, and went swiftly out of harbor and into the glittering waters of the Irish Sea. It was a calm day, and the fast ferry—a catamaran—flew across the water. In half an hour the Wicklow Mountains rose from the horizon, and an hour after that the boat passed the breakwater at Dun Laoghaire and docked. From the ferry terminal it is a ten-minute run on the rapid transit into Dublin's Pearse Street station, and from there a five-minute walk to the Shelbourne Hotel on St. Stephen's Green.

The builders of Russborough, the Leesons, grew rich from property around the green. In 1922 in room 112 of the hotel, Irishmen drafted the constitution that uprooted the last of the hegemony that had supported houses like Russborough. By then the Leesons' treasures had come back down to Dublin, as if summoned in advance by history, and hung in the National Gallery a block from where the family had made its start.

Now the Beits' great hoard of art had been swept from the house and into the National Gallery too. First had come the gift that included the Vermeer, trailing in picture by picture as police retrieved them from Cahill. Then the Belotto and the little Gainsborough. Joining these were the five pictures stolen in the 2002 assault, the fourth, when the Garda found them in a Dublin attic.

The Irish Game

Finally, the Beit Foundation trustees gave up the fight and stripped the last of the paintings from the walls and packed them down to Dublin. Sir Alfred's favorite picture, Gainsborough's *Cottage Girl*, with the adorable child holding a little dog in her arms, arrived in town in the back of a truck. A spokesman at Russborough insisted that, following improvements to security at the house, the pictures would return. In Dublin I found no one who believed it.

That August all of Ireland basked in sunshine. A zephyr plied the green hills. It felt as if the country's crew had hoisted its sails and taken it out to an enchanted sea—the sea of the imagination, where Ireland enacts the splendid theater of itself. In that enraptured moment Russborough's story seemed like a game, sometimes a dark one, to be sure, but perfectly Irish, with the paintings whirling in and out of the house and through the Wicklow Mountains, and the crooks breezing out in a jeep when they wanted more. Built in the Protestant Ascendancy by Protestants in a Catholic country where the Catholics were oppressed—surely a house made by fate to be robbed.

White clouds floated on the hills when I came out to County Wicklow. The palace of Russborough House lay in immaculate light. Behind it the terraces rose up the hill toward Kildare, and a herd of dairy cows grazed at the top.

I took the last tour of the day, and with a few French tourists set out on a walk through the rooms. The guide chattered on about a table set with cutlery that had been a wedding present for the duke of Wellington, and a pair of pianos with matching inlaid rosewood cases, and the ceilings of the Lafrancini brothers. No mention was made of the large, bare patches on the walls and the picture chains that dangled there with nothing on them. The great rooms of the house looked bereft. With the canvases gone, it was easier to notice where cracks had appeared and where the paint was flaking off. In the saloon—the main drawing room—the crimson silk wall covering had faded and was torn. I shifted the drapes to peer out at the steps of the north front, where Cahill had stood in the dark. A row of boulders had been placed across the bottom of the steps, to prevent a vehicle driving up.

There were swans on the water, where the Earl of Milltown had brought the River Liffey from its course to make a pond. His trees raised their massive branches to the Irish sky. Beyond rose the mountains, a granite spine that runs from Dublin Bay to Wexford. The peregrine falcon and the kestrel ride the currents above the bare slopes. Where there are predators, there must be prey.

The Irish Game

Acknowledgments

Two policemen—Liam Hogan and Dick Ellis—helped particularly with the details of the Antwerp sting; my great thanks to both. I owe much to the care, patience, and unfailing warmth of Andrew O'Connor. Thanks also to Sean Feely, Jim Lawlor, Noel Conroy, Brendan Mangan, Valerie Keogh, Raymond Keaveney, Desmond Guinness, the Knight of Glin, and Michael O'Higgins. Special thanks to Pat O'Leary for his help with the details of Rose Dugdale's capture.

I owe much to Jørgen Wadum and Philip Steadman.

My account of *The Scream* could not have come together without the generous assistance of Leif A. Lier and Jørn-Kristian Jørgensen, and the vivid recollections of Einar-Tore Ulving.

In Belgium I had much help from Laurence Massy, Janpiet Callens, and my old friend Tom Peeters.

As always, my deepest gratitude is to my partner, Heather Abbott, who somehow managed, while covering the collapse of Baghdad, to keep me regularly supplied with editorial advice.

Notes

{ 1 } Russborough

Material on the history of Russborough House and the Leesons comes from three sources: Desmond Guinness, *Irish Houses and Castles* (London: Thames and Hudson, 1971); Sergio Benedetti's exhibition catalog *The Milltowns: A Family Reunion* (Dublin: National Gallery of Ireland, 1997); and John Cornforth's article "Russborough, Co. Wicklow" in *Country Life*, December 5, 1963.

The story of the priest at Ballymore Eustace comes from Lorna Siggins's article "Calling Them Obscene Started It All," *Irish Times*, February 2, 1989.

Here, as elsewhere in the book, references to Irish history (e.g., Protestant Ascendancy, Battle of the Boyne) rely on three sources: the 2001 paperback edition of *The Oxford History of Ireland*, ed. R. F. Foster (Oxford: Oxford University Press); Sarah Healy's *A Compact History of Ireland* (Dublin: Mercier Press, 1999); and Richard Killeen's *A Short History of Ireland* (Dublin: Gill and MacMillan, 2001). Killeen's volume was especially useful to an enterprise not scholarly in nature; it divides Irish history into a number of periods and devotes a page or two to each, providing a handy tool for the task of contextualizing a contemporary story in history.

As to the value of the Beits' collection in today's money, such figures are always a little notional, since the only way to get an absolutely reliable figure would be to sell the collection at auction. But if you take the reported figure of eight million pounds for the value of the art taken in 1974 by Dugdale (see discussion in chapter 2) and feed it through online historical currency converters, the result is eighty-five million dollars today. That figure would not include the paintings still in the house or the treasure of silver, porcelain, clocks, furniture, and so on. Art prices rose steeply in the 1980s, so the figure would have moved upward. Another way to reckon the value is to take the Vermeer by itself. *Trace*, a professional art-recovery journal published in London, gives a value (*Trace*, no. 173, July 2003) of three hundred million dollars for the only Vermeer still missing, *The Concert*, stolen in 1990 from Boston's Isabella Stewart Gardner Museum. So the claim of "more than two hundred million dollars" for all the Beit property, which included a Vermeer, is probably conservative.

{ 2 } La Pasionara

I took the details of Rose Dugdale's life from newspaper accounts, including Denis Coughlan's long article "Bridget Rose Dugdale's Road to Limerick Jail," in the *Irish Times*, October 13, 1980, the day after Dugdale's release, and "Cold, Commited and Naïve: The Rose Dugdale I knew," Walter Heaton's memoir of his former lover, as told to David Brazil in the *Irish Press*, November 10, 1977, two days after Heaton's release from an English jail when an appeals court quashed his IRA arms-smuggling conviction. "She was a soft touch . . ." and "She wasn't cold . . ." are from Coughlan's article.

The account of Irish history that sets the scene for the emergence of the IRA is condensed from the three sources listed for chapter 1: Foster, *Oxford History of Ireland*; Healy, *Compact History of Ireland*; and Killeen, *Short History of Ireland*. "At the creek of Baginburn, Ireland was lost and won" is from Killeen's book, page 14.

Details of Dugdale's robbery of her family's property and the ensuing trial, including quotes, are from the *Times* of London editions of October 5, 6, 9, and 23, 1973, and from Coughlan's *Irish Times* profile cited above. Dugdale sought by police after Strabane helicopter bombing: *Times* (London), February 25, 1974.

The account of the robbery, pursuit, and capture of Dugdale is mainly from contemporary editions of the *Irish Times* and from interviews with Chief Superintendent Sean Feely and retired Garda sergeant Pat O'Leary. Material on the Garda itself is from *An Garda Síochána: Ireland's Police Force*, a booklet produced by the Garda's community relations section in 1995.

{ 3 } Under the Overpaint

I spoke to the knight of Glin in London. "Vermeer madness" was a coinage of the Dutch press. The public appetite for Vermeer is supported by the attendance figures. The Washington show ran for seventy days and drew 327,551 visitors. Compare with the show of Michaelangelo drawings later in 1996, which ran sixty-nine days and drew 94,882. For the value of a Vermeer, see the reference to *Trace* in the notes for chapter 1. Also, in "Time Is on Side of Gardner Art Thieves," Daniel Golden, *Boston Globe*, December 16, 1994, uses three hundred million dollars as a value for the stolen Gardner works (see chapter 7). The Vermeer is always understood to account for the greatest part of such figures. I interviewed the detective Laurence Massy in Brussels. Arthur Wheelock's "part of the package" remark was made to me during a telephone interview.

My account of Vermeer's life is taken mainly from Anthony Bailey's *Vermeer, a View of Delft* (New York: Henry Holt, 2001), but I also kept on hand *The Cambridge Companion to Vermeer*, ed. Wayne E. Franits (Cambridge University Press, 2001), and

Norbert Schneider's *Vermeer: The Complete Paintings*, translated by Fiona Hulse (Cologne: Benedikt Taschen, 2000). "At once dreamlike and real . . . stiller and more serene" is from Michiko Kakutani's review of *Vermeer, a View of Delft* in the *New York Times*, March 20, 2001.

The story of Andrew O'Connor's discovery of the seal in the foreground of *Lady Writing a Letter with Her Maid* comes from O'Connor himself, who consulted his own notes. I also looked at his "A Note on the Beit Vermeer" in the *Burlington Magazine*, April 1977. All details of the O'Connor family are from O'Connor.

As to the meaning of the discovery, see *Johannes Vermeer*, the catalog issued by the National Gallery of Art, Washington, and Royal Cabinet of Paintings Mauritshuis, The Hague (Waanders: Zwolle, 1995). "One allusion to the mistress' concerns is found on the black and white marble floor just before her writing table: a crumpled letter. As a red wax seal also lies on the floor, the letter must be one she had received rather than a discarded draft of the one she composes. Letters were highly valued and not objects to be thrown aside, except, perhaps, in anger," pages 187–88 of the catalog.

{ 4 } The General

Any account of Cahill's life and crimes must lean upon Dublin crime reporter Paul Williams's *The General: Godfather of Crime* (Dublin: O'Brien Press, 1995), and much of the material in this chapter comes from this book. Equally important are two long articles by Michael O'Higgins in the Irish current-affairs monthly *Magill*: "The General," March 1988, and "Of Mice and Men," July 1988. O'Higgins spent long hours in private, face-to-face interviews with Cahill, which formed the main basis for his articles, and I prefer him on the General's personal psychology, for example, on the evolution of Cahill's personality and behavior at St. Conleth's and Mountjoy. I look to Williams for details that must have come either from police or from criminal sources other than Cahill, such as the construction of a bunker in the Wicklow Mountains before the Beit robbery.

I consulted the *Irish Times* and the *Irish Independent* too frequently to cite each instance, but I record my gratitude to Jim Cusack, the security correspondent of the former, for meeting with me and discussing Cahill. Cusack's opinion of the criminal is exemplified in "More Like a General Gouger," *Irish Times*, February 11, 1999, in which he firmly rejects the idea that Cahill was any kind of Robin Hood.

The quote from James Joyce's story "A Little Cloud" is from p. 66 of *Dubliners*, London: Penguin Books, 2000.

Details of Cahill's approach to the house are from Feely. O'Shea account is from garda Jim Lawlor and Feely.

{ 5 } Stalking Cahill

Jettisoning pictures is from Sean Flynn, "Paintings Worth over 10 Million Pounds Stolen from Beit Home," *Irish Times*, May 22, 1986. (Value climbing to thirty million by the second sentence.) The incident on Terenure Road is from Williams, *The General*. "I

cannot think other . . . for the state" is from Flynn, "Paintings." The difficulty of disposing of stolen high-end art is a commonplace among detectives. See also Peter Wat-
son, "Stolen Art: The Unromantic Truth," *Times* (London), August 29, 2003.

For Charley Hill's recovery of the Titian, see Sarah Lyall, "A Titian Is No
Longer at Large; Its Thief Is," *New York Times*, September 19, 2002. "I daresay he
covered his expenses" is from an interview with Mark Dalrymple, Tyler & Co.,
London, chartered loss adjusters. Details of Hill's personal life are from Hill, but
see also John Wilson, "Watching the Detective," *Observer* (London), August 5, 2001,
and Colin Gleadell, "The Art Detective," *Telegraph* (London), July 8, 2002. The
account of Hill's operations is from Hill, Dick Ellis, and Liam Hogan. Details on
O'Shea and the statues are from Siggins, "Calling Them Obscene Started It All,"
with additional information from Matthew Hart, "Billionaires, Burglars and Bun-
glers," *Domino* (Toronto; *Globe and Mail*), November 1990.

Cahill riding high is from O'Higgins ("Of Mice and Men," pp. 18 and 19). Irish
attitude toward law is my own paraphrase of a point made repeatedly by various
sources. City of London dealer is from Ellis. Information on Van Scoaik is from
Williams, *The General*, with some details from O'Higgins.

{ 6 } The Tango Squad

Six hundred robberies is from Williams, *The General*. Cahill slipping his surveillance is
from ibid. and O'Higgins. Weekly meetings, South African spies, and "Youse made a
mistake . . ." are from Williams, *The General*. Some material on Doherty is from ibid.
and O'Higgins ("Of Mice and Men"). Garda crisis, appointment of Wren and
Doherty, and Doherty's succession are from O'Higgins ibid.

The *Eksund* incident appears in Williams, *The General*, and O'Higgins, but I take
my account from Ed Moloney's *A Secret History of the IRA* (Norton: New York, 2002).
The IRA's "few committed members" and the demise of the Harrison network are
from Moloney, *Secret History of the IRA*. The raid by police and troops is from ibid. and
Williams, *The General*. (Williams says fifty thousand locations; Moloney, sixty thousand. I prefer Moloney because his work is documented.)

The Doherty meeting, the Kilnamanagh robbery, Ned Ryan's rage, and the establishment of the Tango squad are from Williams, *The General*. Most of the material on
Noel Conroy is from ibid. Conroy's reputation is from Hogan, and Cusack in conversation. (All references to Hogan in these notes mean Liam Hogan.) Gardaí training
for Tango operations and approach to Cahill are from Williams, *The General*. Breathalyzer test on Daly and slashed tires are from ibid. and O'Higgins ("Of Mice and
Men"). "Martin, me old flower . . ." is from Williams, *The General*. Balance of Tango
activity is from ibid., O'Higgins, Hogan, Cusack, and Conroy. Spike Island is from
O'Higgins and Williams, *The General*, and John Cahill getting sixteen years is from
Williams, *The General*. That the Beit collection was an albatross for Cahill is heard on
every hand among police and reporters.

The Murnaghan robbery is mainly from Williams, *The General*. An acquaintance of the family told me that the venerable lady smoked and liked to read late. Naughton is from Williams, *The General*, and Ellis.

Tommy Coyle's involvement in the UVF deal is from Cusack and Williams, *The General*. Cusack refers to him as "the man in Drogheda" and Williams as "the fence from Drogheda." Coyle died in 2000, and his identity was put in the public realm. See Elaine Keogh and Jim Cusack, "Biggest 'Fence' in Irish History Dies," *Irish Times*, September 20, 2000. Cusack in penultimate citation does not say loyalists were UVF, but Williams and Conroy assert it.

The dense population of spies and terrorists comes from numerous anecdotes and remarks of policemen and journalists, but see, for example, Rosie Cowan, "Ulster Spies to 'Blow MI5 Cover,'" *Guardian*, July 6, 2002, and Henry McDonald, "Terrorists Reach the Crossroads," *Observer*, October 17, 1999. For Sinn Féin and the peace process, see, for example, Sinn Féin leader Gerry Adams's speech on disarmament as reprinted in the *Guardian*, April 28, 2003, the day after he gave it. That the UVF deal damaged Cahill's reputation is from Williams, *The General*, Frank Doherty, and Paddy Prendeville. The return of the Metsu is from O'Connor.

{ 7 } Mrs. Gardner's House

The account of the Gardners comes from Louise Hall Tharp, *Mrs. Jack: A Biography of Isabella Stewart Gardner* (Boston: Little, Brown, 1965).

The account of the robbery, including quotes, is assembled from numerous reports in the *Boston Globe*. See, for example, Andy Dabilis and John Ellement, "$200 Million Gardner Museum Art Theft, Two Men Posing as Police Tie Up Night Guards," March 19, 1990; Elizabeth Neuffer, "Inch by Inch, Hunt for Clues Goes On," March 21, 1990; Elizabeth Neuffer, "Gardner: Masterworks of Crime. Retracing the Steps of Robbery's Twisted Trail," May 13, 1990; Elizabeth Neuffer, "FBI Is Said to Have Suspects Worldwide in Gardner Theft," May 14, 1990.

For details of FBI suspects, go to www.fbi.gov, type *Gardner* into the search field, then scroll down to *Seeking Information* and select the Gardner robbery. For Brian McDevitt, see Brian McGrory, "Gardner Art Theft Suspect Is Study in Intrigue," *Boston Globe*, June 3, 1992, and Shelley Murphy and Zachary Dowdy, "Screenwriter Questioned in Gardner Museum Heist," *Boston Globe*, August 7, 1993.

The account of the life of Myles Connor, Jr., comes from numerous sources. See, for example, Elizabeth Neuffer, "Myles Connor Sentenced to 20 Years," *Boston Globe*, July 17, 1990; Steve Lopez, "The Great Art Caper," *Time*, November 17, 1997; William M. Carley, "Easel Pickings: For This Art Collector, Priceless Paintings Are Get-Out-Of-Jail Cards," *Wall Street Journal*, September 29, 1997; Tom Mashberg, "Stealing Beauty," *Vanity Fair*, March 1998. An Internet site, www.e-vent.com, has "The History of Boston Rock & Roll," and chapter 6 includes details of Connor's brushes with the law. Connor's description of the theft of a Rembrandt from Boston's Museum of Fine Arts comes from my interview with Connor.

The William P. Youngworth III episode is from, for example, Scott Baldauf, "Museum Asks: Does It Take a Thief to Catch a Degas?" *Christian Science Monitor*, August

29, 1997; Stephen Kurkjian and Judy Rakowlsky, "Report Reignites Art Heist Probe: Officials Approach Reporter, 2 Others," *Boston Globe*, August 28, 1997. Mashberg's warehouse adventure, including quotes, is from Mashberg, "Stealing Beauty." Stern is from a telephone interview with me.

Transatlantic underworld connections are from Ellis and Hogan. Montreal incident is from my telephone interview with Denis Bergeron, a former Montreal detective now with the Sûreté du Québec. The *Time* quote is from Lopez, "The Great Art Caper." Kevin Cullen is from a telephone interview. Bulger on wanted list may be viewed at www.fbi.gov. The Connolly trial is amply reported. See, for example, Shelley Murphy, "Jury Is Told of Bribes from Bulger," *Boston Globe*, May 9, 2002, and Andrea Estes, "Conviction of Ex-agent Upheld," *Boston Globe*, August 15, 2003. The Hill quote is from a telephone interview.

The "Turbo" story is from Ellis. Larry Potts's retention by the Gardner and Youngworth's letter to Potts are from an Associated Press story reprinted at www.museum-security.org.

{ 8 } Liam's Game

Liam Hogan's biography is from Hogan. Limerick's sieges are in the above-cited historical works and numerous Web sites, such as www.irelandonthenet.ie and www.limerick corp.ie. Secret societies are from Killeen, *Short History of Ireland*, Mountbatten and ambush of paratroopers are from Moloney, *Secret History of the IRA*. Coyle as snout is from my conversations with Hogan and with Williams.

New attempt to move Beit collection and its movement to England is from Hogan and Ellis. Subsequent thefts and raids are from Ellis. Movement to Antwerp is from Hogan and Ellis. John Butler's reasoning is from my interview with Butler. Development of sting is from Hogan, Ellis, and Hill. The mechanics of the sting is from Hogan, Ellis, Butler, and Hill, with some help from Janpiet Callens of the art and antiques unit of the Belgian federal police. See also Veronica Guerin, "Beit Sting: The Inside Story," *Sunday Tribune*, September 5, 1993, for some details on Niall Mulvihill.

The art-for-drugs scheme is from Hogan, Ellis, Butler, and Hill, but see Martin Bailey, "The Art Theft–Drug Smuggling Link Exposed," *Art Newspaper*, January 1997.

{ 9 } In Vermeer

Transfer of pictures to museum is from many sources, including Hogan, O'Connor, and Liesbeth Schotsman, registrar, Koninklijk Meseum voor Schone Kunsten. Dinner with Patrick Cradock and arrival to secure pictures is from O'Connor. The Jørgen Wadum sketch is from Wadum. Preparations had begun for Vermeer show is from O'Connor, Wadum, and Ben Broos. The Proust quote and account of Wadum's restoration of *The Girl with the Pearl Earring* are from *Vermeer Illuminated*, Wadum's booklet on the work, published undated by the Mauritshuis. Wadum's developing interest in perspective, arrival at museum, and discovery of pinhole are from Wadum. For a fuller account of Wadum's theory, see his "Vermeer in Perspective" in *Johannes Vermeer*, the catalog of the 1995–96 Vermeer show cited in the notes for chapter 3.

The camera obscura account, including historical quotes, is from Philip Steadman, *Vermeer's Camera: Uncovering the Truth Behind the Masterpieces* (Oxford: Oxford University Press, 2001), and from my interview with Steadman. Wheelock's reservations are from his "Vermeer of Delft: His Life and His Artistry," in the cited catalog of the 1995–96 show.

The return of the Vermeer to Dublin and Lord Gowrie's gift are from O'Connor. The Hogans' dialogue is from Liam Hogan.

{ 10 } The Scream

The account of the theft and recovery of *The Scream* comes from my personal reporting in Norway as to descriptions of locale. All details of the theft and sting are from my interviews with Leif A. Lier, Ellis, Butler, Hill, and Stein-Morten Lier and Einar-Tore Ulving.

{ 11 } The Irish Game

Cahill's desperation as evidenced by plans to steal Book of Kells is from Williams, *The General*. For a digest of IRA cease-fire talks, including Downing Street Declaration, see www.bbc.co.uk. Widow Scallans, IRA agent, Cahill assassination, and funeral are from Williams, *The General*.

The Russborough robberies of 2001 and 2002 are from Feely and numerous newspaper accounts, such as the following, all from the *Irish Times*: Eoin Burke-Kennedy, "Hunt Continues After £3M Art Theft from Russborough House," June 26, 2001; Edward Power, "Gardaí Recover Stolen Beit Masterpieces from Dublin House," September 27, 2002; Joe Humphreys, "Russborough's Security to Be Discussed after Latest Robbery," October 1, 2002; Tim O'Brien, "Russborough Closes as Beit Collection Paintings Removed," October 5, 2002. The details of Guerin's license plate are from Hogan.

The Shelbourne has a plaque on the door of the room where the constitution was drafted.

Index

Harald, king of Norway, 166
Harcourt Square, 85, 127, 129
Harley-Davidson motorcycle, 45, 48, 89
Harmony in Blue and Silver, Trouville
    (Whistler), 103
Harrison, George, 82
Harvard College, 107–8
Harward, Billy, 174–75
Hayes, Con, 20, 21, 22, 23
Heaton, Walter, 7–8, 9–10, 11, 17
Heavy Gang, 44, 81
Hill, Charley, 60–65, 121, 137–38, 139,
    142, 143, 144
  left Scotland Yard, 185
  sting in *The Scream* theft, 172, 174, 175,
    176, 177, 178, 179, 181, 182, 183
  succeeded Butler at Scotland Yard,
    185
  verifying the art, 140–41
Hogan, Eileen, 124
Hogan, Liam, 122, 123–25, 124f, 126,
    127–30, 131, 137, 140, 164
  bringing Beit paintings home,
    162–63
  made inspector, 185
  and recovery of *Lady Writing . . .* ,
    141–42, 143–44
  sting, 129–33
Hogan, Ned, 17, 18, 19, 21, 25f, 123,
    124–25, 141, 164
Hogan, Shavo, 70, 74, 75, 76, 85, 89
  and movement of Beit paintings,
    134
Holbein, Hans, xi
Hollyfield Buildings, 42, 44, 45, 46
Hollywood, 190
Holyhead, 193
Home rule, 9
Horrigan, James, 12, 13
Hooch, Pieter de, 153
Houckgeest, Gerard, 153
How to Win Friends and Influence People
    (Carnegie), 43
Hyde Collection Art Museum, 111

Inchicore, 83
Inconceivability test, 136
Informants, 58, 59
  in Cahill's gang, 95
  lies told by, 131–32
  in Oslo, 172
  regarding Beit collection, 17–18, 130
Insurance/insurers, xii, 110, 136
Intelligence, 95
  exchange of, 130
  Israeli, 168–69
  Scotland Yard's concern with, 131
Interior paintings, 152–53, 158
Interpol, 7, 74, 96, 139
IRA
  see Irish Republican Army (IRA)
Ireland
  attitude to authority, 67, 126
  crime in, 78, 82–83, 127, 129
  criminal trade, 117
  fell to prince of Orange, 126
  outlaw groups and agents, 96
  republic, 9
  union of, 9, 82
Irish criminals
  contest with police, 189–93
Irish game, 186–95
Irish gangs
  in Leighton Buzzard, 132–33
  in New England, 64
  in sting, 136, 137, 138, 139, 140, 142,
    144, 170
Irish government
  and peace in Northern Ireland, 96
Irish history, 8–9
Irish Independent, 192
Irish Republican Army (IRA), 8, 9, 15,
    16, 21, 24, 45, 76, 81, 93, 96, 97, 126,
    147 186
  American Irish support for, 117
  bombings, 126–27
  and Cahill, 94, 187–88
  declined Beit paintings, 94, 59
  Dugdale's connection to, 32

Index

www.randomhouse.co.uk/vintage